Arise & Pray:
A 100-Day Journey to
Spiritual Renewal

Copyright Notice

First edition published 2025
Printed and distributed by Amazon KDP
ISBN: 9798297755505

For permissions, bulk purchases, or church licensing inquiries, please contact: **ukpcea@gmail.com**

This book is a product of the 100 Days of Prayer campaign; birthed within UK PCEA, supported by the Adult Youth Ministry, Evangelism Committee, and Kirk Session, and written and compiled by the UK PCEA Youth Pastor.

This book is intended for spiritual growth and edification. The views expressed herein are those of the author and do not necessarily represent the official stance of any institution or organisation. The author and publisher are not liable for any misinterpretation or misuse of the content.

Table of Contents

Dedication

To our Lord and Saviour, Jesus Christ,
who called us out of darkness into His marvellous light.
Your grace sustains us, Your truth guides us,
and Your presence is our greatest joy.
May this book bring glory to Your name
and draw many closer to You.

Contributors

This book was made possible through the efforts of many individuals who shared their insights, prayers, and experiences. Special thanks to:

John Mwithiga – For creating the daily themes and accompanying scriptures and his "Lessons in Prayer", which have been adapted and interspersed throughout the book.

Rev. Jesse Munyoroku – For his foreword and unwavering and visionary support. Your leadership and encouragement have been instrumental in this entire journey.

Acknowledgments

We extend our deepest gratitude to:

John Mwithiga, Dorcas Kinyua, Lilian Wachira, and the Milton Keynes youth team, from whom the seed of the 100-day prayer season was sown. Your faith and initiative inspired this movement.

The UK PCEA Adult Youth Committee (2024-25), and our Youth Patron, for championing and representing the vision to the church and leading by example.

The facilitators and members of UK PCEA and all who joined the 100-day morning prayer calls—your dedication, commitment, and hunger for God encouraged and strengthened us all.

May the fruits of this book continue to transform lives, fuel Christian mission, and bring us ever closer to God's presence.

Foreword by Rev. Jesse Munyoroku

The 100 Days of Prayer journey in UK PCEA has been a remarkable journey of faith, devotion, and transformation. Our final day's theme, "Finishing Grace," encapsulated the spirit of perseverance that carried us through this sacred season. It reminded us of the power of prayer as captured in the song we sang so often, which started in the Milton Keynes congregation:

"Prayer is the key,
Prayer is the key,
Prayer is the Master's key.
Jesus started with prayers and ended with prayers;
Prayer is the Master's key."

This season of prayer was a time to be revived, refreshed, rekindled, restored, recharged, and reproved in righteousness. Each morning, we were greeted with a simple yet profound reminder: "The throne room is always open for prayer. When you come to God, believe that He is, and that He rewards those who diligently seek Him." This echoes the promise in Jeremiah 29:13: "You will seek me and find me when you seek me with all your heart."

The *100 Days of Prayer* was not an easy journey—it required commitment, confession, dedication, obedience, and consecration through faith. It was a spiritual battle, as we fought the works of the enemy through the mandate in Jeremiah 1:10: *"See, I have set you this day over nations and over kingdoms, to pluck up and to break down, to destroy and to overthrow, to build and to plant."* Together, we uprooted sin, tore down strongholds, and rebuilt lives in the foundation of Christ.

I want to take this moment to congratulate and thank everyone who participated so faithfully in this journey of prayer. Special thanks go to the Youth Ministry leadership, the organising committee, and the facilitators who led us with such dedication. May the Lord richly bless you for your labour in His vineyard.

The central purpose of calling the church to this season of prayer was to cleanse the temple of the Lord, which is our bodies, from sin and idolatry. It was a call to give Jesus Christ His rightful place in our lives so that He might reign supreme. Throughout these 100 days, we were reminded of the importance of prayer and its transformative power. We learned the value of praying with scripture, anchoring our petitions in the promises of God, which are ours through Christ.

During this time, we built deeper relationships with God, made our petitions known to Him, and gave thanks for answered prayers. We stayed focused on what truly matters, holding on to hope even in dark times. Prayer helped us remain connected to God on a deeper level, keeping our minds clear and our hearts compassionate. It brought comfort, peace, and strength to our lives and helped us grow as a community of faith.

One of the most profound lessons we learned was that prayer is not just an act of communication but an opportunity to co-labour with God. Through prayer, we allow Him to express His desires through us and accomplish His purposes.

On Day 74, we experienced a powerful breakthrough when the Holy Spirit moved mightily among us. Many received the gift of the Spirit and began to speak in tongues, marking a turning point in our journey. From that moment, the prayers rose to a new level, and participation continued to grow, day by day.

Today, we celebrate the Lord's faithfulness with testimonies and thanksgiving offerings. As we reflect on what God has done, I urge the church to remain steadfast in prayer and fellowship, encouraging one another and carrying each other's burdens as intercessors. Hebrews 10:25 reminds us, *"Not neglecting to meet together, as is the habit of some, but encouraging one another, and all the more as you see the Day drawing near."*

James 4:8 reminds us of this truth: *"Draw near to God, and He will draw near to you."* The more time we spend in prayer, the closer we grow to Him, and the deeper our faith becomes.

As we look to the future, we look to the One whom we imitate—Jesus Christ—the ultimate prayer warrior and intercessor who continues to pray for us at the throne of grace today. The Apostle Paul's words to the Thessalonians provide the perfect charge for us: "Rejoice always, pray without ceasing, give thanks in all circumstances; for this is the will of God in Christ Jesus for you. Do not quench the Spirit. Do not despise prophecies, but test everything; hold fast what is good. Abstain from every form of evil." (1 Thessalonians 5:16-22).

May God Himself, the God of peace, sanctify you through and through. May your whole spirit, soul, and body be kept blameless at the coming of our Lord Jesus Christ. (1 Thessalonians 5:23).

Arise and Shine, Glorify Christ!

Rev. Jesse Munyoroku

Parish Minister
UK Presbyterian Church of East Africa (UK P.C.E.A.)

Arise! Shine! Glorify Christ!

The 2025 annual theme for UK PCEA is Arise! Shine! Glorify Christ! Which comes from Isaiah 60:1-3, *"Arise, shine, for your light has come, and the glory of the LORD has risen upon you. For behold, darkness shall cover the earth, and thick darkness the peoples; but the LORD will arise upon you, and His glory will be seen upon you. And nations shall come to your light, and kings to the brightness of your rising."*

The Prophet Isaiah's message is one of hope, comfort, and forgiveness. Speaking during a time of national spiritual decay, Isaiah called Judah to repentance and faithfulness to God. He reminded them that sacrifices and worship mean nothing if not accompanied by acts of humility, justice, and care for the vulnerable, as God commanded in Isaiah 1:10-17. This same prophetic call echoes to us today: a call to live lives that honour God and reflect His light in a world filled with darkness.

Isaiah's prophecy found its ultimate fulfilment in the coming of Jesus Christ, the Messiah. He is the Light of the World, as He declared in John 8:12: *"I am the light of the world. Whoever follows me will never walk in darkness but will have the light of life."*

Through Christ, the glory of God has risen upon us, and His light now shines in and through His people. This truth comes with a divine mandate for every believer:

Bring Light to the Darkness – We are called to be bearers of God's light in a world filled with spiritual blindness and hopelessness. This involves speaking the truth, offering hope, and extending God's love to those in need.

Reflect Light in the World – As believers, our lives must reflect the light of Christ through our attitudes, actions, and words. This is not just about personal transformation but about being an example for others to follow.

Bring Glory to God's Name Through Good Deeds – Jesus reminds us in Matthew 5:16: *"Let your light shine before others, so that they may see your good works and give glory to your Father who is in heaven."* Every good deed we do must point back to the greatness of God, drawing people closer to Him.

Fulfil the Great Commission – Our light is not to remain hidden; it is to go out into all nations, as Jesus commands in Matthew 28:19-20: *"Go therefore and make disciples of all nations, baptising them in the name of the Father and of the Son and of the Holy Spirit, teaching them to observe all that I have commanded you."*

The theme challenges us to ask: **Are you ready to be used by God?** In 2025, we are called to rise above complacency, shine the light of Christ in every area of life, and glorify His name in all that we do. As we live out this theme, may we embody the hope of Isaiah's prophecy, reflect Christ's radiance, and draw many to the brightness of His light.

Spiritual Formation in Young People

In his message "Where Jesus Travels," David Mathis emphasises the importance of the means of grace—God's appointed ways through which believers experience His life-giving presence[1]. For young people in the church, engaging with these means is vital for nurturing a deep connection with God.

Mathis uses the analogy of faucets and light switches to explain how the means of grace function. Just as water flows when a faucet is turned on and light fills a room when a switch is flipped, God's grace is abundantly available, but we must position ourselves to receive it. This involves *actively* engaging in the practices God has established as conduits of His grace.

When engaging young people in Christian youth ministry in our modern world, it is easy to fall into the trap of believing that events, programs, and innovations alone will build true disciples of Jesus Christ. By actively engaging in these means of grace, young people can position themselves to receive the fullness of God's life-transforming presence, much like opening a faucet to receive water or flipping a switch to illuminate a room.

While the UK PCEA Adult Youth Ministry has been a hub of activity—organising events like worship experiences, missions to various UK cities, weekend retreats, the launch of a brand-new podcast, and more—it became clear by mid-2024 that we were at risk of prioritising busyness over spiritual depth and richness. The feedback from our last major youth ministry activity, the 2024 youth retreat, was a wake-up call. A collective cry arose from the youth for something deeper: a real, sustained connection with God through prayer.

---

[1] Mathis, D., 2024. *Where Jesus Travels: Introducing the Means of Grace.* [Online] Available at: https://www.desiringgod.org/messages/where-jesus-travels [Accessed 22 February 2025].

Taking an inventory of which *means of grace* already yielded fruit in connecting us with God's presence was our weekly Bible studies; reading and discussing a chapter a week. Since late 2021, our Bible reading initiatives have been fruitful, yielding real spiritual understanding in the youth ministry. Realising and focusing this, we fully understood that sustained prayer was the next priority. We needed to elevate prayer to the same level of importance and activity in the youth ministry to drive forward the spiritual formation of our young people to grow upward in Christ.

The seed for *100 Days of Prayer* was sown within our Milton Keynes youth team. During a virtual leadership check-in, the team shared the beginning of their prayer journey. It was inspiring to see their daily structure, planning tools, and overall strategy take shape. What was initially planned for two weeks ended up lasting twelve! It was there that the embers of a national prayer season were ignited.

Gimmicks Versus Genuine Encounters

This campaign for 100 days of prayer was a response to that need—to kick start our prayer life toward a deeper life with Christ Jesus. It was not about adding another program or event to our calendar but about creating a sacred space for encountering God in His fullness. Brian H. Cosby observed that many youth ministries rely too much on entertainment and "attraction" methods to engage young people today. He concludes that such approaches provide only temporary and superficial satisfaction, failing to address deeper spiritual formation needs. This reliance on gimmicks can leave students spiritually unfulfilled and disconnected from authentic faith experiences[2]. I agree with him, there is a need for "substance over style" in youth ministry efforts today.

---

[2] Cosby, B.H. (2012) *Giving Up Gimmicks: Reclaiming Youth Ministry from an Entertainment Culture*. Phillipsburg, NJ: P&R Publishing.

Gimmicks, while creative and engaging, cannot produce true disciples. Only through a genuine encounter with the presence of God, experienced in His prescribed way, can lives be transformed and faith deepened.

There are no shortcuts in spiritual growth. While events and initiatives have their place in bringing people together, they must always lead to something greater: an abiding relationship with Jesus Christ. This season of prayer reminded us that more than activity, we need God's presence. It is only in His presence that we are refreshed, renewed, and shaped into true disciples.

Igniting the Path to God's Presence

The Bible prescribes experiencing God's presence through means of grace. The following are four of the many means I'd like to explore: Praise and worship, reading scripture, being in community, and prayer.

Praise and Worship

Worship allows us to enter into God's presence with reverence and gratitude. Psalm 100:4 calls us to *"enter his gates with thanksgiving, and his courts with praise! Give thanks to him; bless his name!"*

This verse shows how praise and thanksgiving open the door to a deeper experience of God's presence. Worship is not limited to words but includes singing, as we come before Him with joyful hearts.

1 Corinthians 14:15 encourages us to embrace both our spirit and understanding in worship: *"I will pray with my spirit, but I will pray with my mind also; I will sing praise with my spirit, but I will sing with my mind also."*

Incorporating spiritual gifts, like speaking in tongues, in private worship helps us engage with God on a deeper, more personal level. Worship transforms our hearts, aligns us with God's will, and brings us closer to Him.

Reading Scripture

Scripture, too, is a vital means of experiencing God's presence. 2 Timothy 3:16-17 declares, *"All Scripture is breathed out by God and profitable for teaching, for reproof, for correction, and for training in righteousness, that the man of God may be complete, equipped for every good work."* To say Scripture is God-breathed is to acknowledge that it originates from God Himself, carrying His wisdom and authority – His very presence.

When you immerse yourself in the Word, you encounter God's voice speaking directly into your life. Reading Scripture is more than an intellectual exercise; it is a spiritual practice that transforms you, drawing you closer to Him when you focus on enjoying God and feeding on the flesh of Jesus. Allow the living Word to guide you, shape you, and fill you with His presence as you spend time with Him through the pages of the Bible.

Being in Community

God's presence is often experienced most profoundly when we gather together as believers. Psalm 22:3 reminds us that God is enthroned on the praises of His people, showing us that collective worship creates a space where His presence dwells.

Remember the account in Exodus 24:9-12, *"the 70 elders of Israel saw God"? "Under his feet was something like a pavement made of lapis lazuli, as bright blue as the sky"*. As the elders ate and fellowshipped together, God's presence was there.

Hebrews 2:12 reinforces this truth of what Jesus does today when His people are in community, saying, *"I will tell of your name to my brothers; in the midst of the congregation, I will sing your praise."* What God did with the fellowship of elders on the mountain, He will do today amongst the fellowship of believers in the church. To think even Jesus sings with us when we come together to worship Him is an incredible promise of God's presence!

When we come together as a community, we not only worship God but also encourage and uplift one another, uniting our hearts in His presence. Jesus Himself declared in Matthew 18:20, *"For where two or three are gathered in my name, there am I among them."* Being in community strengthens our faith, keeps us accountable, and reminds us that we are not alone on the path of discipleship. God designed us to walk this journey together, sharing in both joys and challenges, so we might grow deeper in our experience of His love and grace.

Prayer

Prayer is a powerful means of experiencing God's presence and participating in His divine plan. While prayer does not change God's eternal decrees, it is the instrument through which He gloriously brings them about.

Scripture teaches that prayer has the ability to stir hearts, change circumstances, and align us with God's will. James 5:16 reminds us, *"The prayer of a righteous person has great power as it is working,"* demonstrating how God uses the prayers of His people to accomplish His purposes. As you *actively* work God's will in prayer, His power is released. Elijah's prayer in James 5:17–18 changed the course of events, proving the power of prayer in influencing circumstances within God's providential design.

Prayer is also a means of transformation. In Luke 18:2–6, Jesus teaches the importance of persistence in prayer, encouraging us to remain steadfast, trusting that God hears and responds in His perfect way. Jesus Himself modelled prayer's intensity in Luke 22:44, where He prayed with such fervency that His sweat became like drops of blood.

Prayer not only affects events but also changes us. It deepens our intimacy with God, shapes our desires to reflect His, and strengthens our faith as we depend on Him so taking personal inventory of your prayer life is essential. When prayer takes its rightful place in your life, you will discover it is not just a practice but a pathway to encounter the fullness of God's presence and purpose.

Where can you take personal inventory of your Christian life and elevate prayer to the highest place today?

Solomon's Temple

Creating a high-place of worship of Jesus in our lives is the main focus here. Biblically, there was no higher sacred place in ancient Old Testament biblical times than the Tabernacle - designed by God and built by Moses. Later on, in the time of the Kings, King Solomon built the next iteration of Moses' Tabernacle called Solomon's Temple. 1 Kings 6 provides a detailed description of Solomon's Temple, capturing its grandeur and intricate design.

The temple measured approximately 27.8 metres in length, 9.3 metres in width, and 13.9 metres in height. Its layout featured a prominent eastern entrance, reflecting its orientation and symbolic significance. The structure was built with precision, using stone, cedar, and gold to create a sanctuary worthy of God's presence.

Externally, the walls were crafted from finely cut stone and lined with cedar, which was richly adorned with carvings of cherubim, palm trees, and open flowers. These designs brought a sense of life and reverence to the sacred space. The roof, supported by sturdy cedar beams, was also overlaid with gold, highlighting the temple's unmatched splendour.

Around the temple, there were additional chambers built in three stories, providing storage and functional space for the temple's operations. A winding staircase connected the levels, demonstrating the thoughtful and practical design of the structure. High windows lined the walls, allowing light to filter in while maintaining the sanctity of the interior.

The temple featured a porch at the entrance, 9.3 metres wide and 4.6 metres deep. This porch included two bronze pillars named Jachin and Boaz, each standing approximately 8.3 metres tall and crowned with intricate capitals. These pillars were both decorative and symbolic, representing strength and stability in God's covenant with His people.

Internally, the temple was divided into two primary sections: the Holy Place and the Most Holy Place. The Holy Place measured 18.5 metres in length and was the larger of the two chambers. The Most Holy Place, also known as the inner sanctuary, formed a perfect cube, measuring 9.3 metres in length, width, and height. Every inch of the interior walls was covered in gold, and the floor was laid with gold boards, creating an atmosphere of overwhelming majesty.

In the Most Holy Place, two large cherubim made of olive wood and overlaid with gold stood as guardian angels of the Ark of the Covenant, their wings stretched across the room, emphasising the holiness of the space.

One notable aspect of the temple's design is the lack of significant detail regarding a western gate. While the eastern entrance is described in detail, there is little mention of an equivalent feature on the western side. The little mention of the western side of the temple is found in 1 Chronicles 26:16.

We read that the West Gate and the Shallecheth Gate were assigned to Shuppim and Hosah from the house of Merari, the tribe of Levi.

So, what can we learn from scripture about this side of the temple?

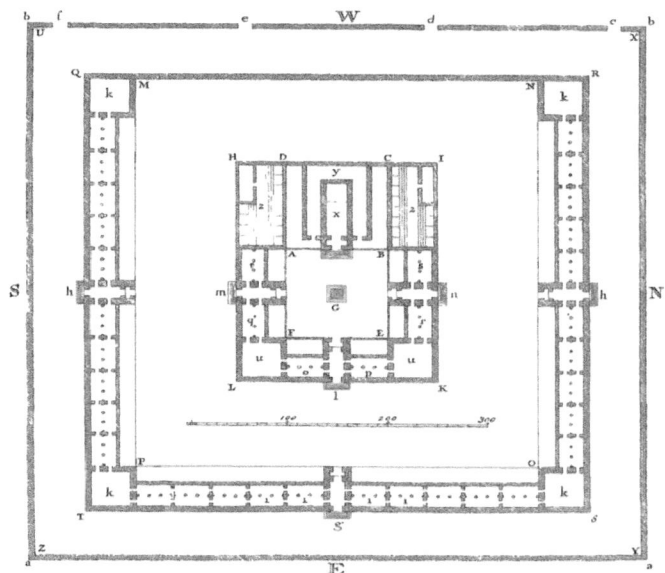

Figure 1:
A blueprint of the Temple of Solomon. Along the Western wall: c. The Gate Shallecheth; d. The Gate Parbar; e.f. The two Gates Assupim.

The West Gate – A Call to Prayer and Renewal

The significance of the West Gate is deeply rooted in biblical symbolism and its connection to God's redemptive work.

Also known as the Shallecheth Gate (see fig. 1), which translates to "the gate of casting out[3]," it was located on the ascending highway and served as the exit for the ashes, refuse, and waste from the temple operations and rituals[4]. This gate, positioned behind the Holy of Holies, led out to a causeway that connected to the Parbar, an open-space or "suburb"[5] used by temple officials for various functions.

Purity and Security

The imagery of this gate speaks to the process of purification and removal of what is unclean from a sacred space. This physical act points to the spiritual work of God in cleansing and renewing His people. Isaiah 59:19 highlights this when it says, *"So shall they fear the name of the LORD from the west, and His glory from the rising of the sun; when the enemy comes in like a flood, the Spirit of the LORD will lift up a standard against him."* From the west, where cleansing began, God's glory was to arise and bring deliverance.

The gatekeepers played a crucial role in preserving order, regulating access, and safeguarding the sanctity of the temple. The specific mention of Shallecheth in the division of gatekeepers emphasises its significance within the temple's overall design and function.

---

[3] NAS Exhaustive Concordance of the Bible with Hebrew-Aramaic and Greek Dictionaries. Copyright © 1981, 1998 by The Lockman Foundation

[4] Bible Hub, 2024. *Topical Encyclopaedia: Shallecheth.* [Online] Available at: https://biblehub.com/topical/s/shallecheth.htm [Accessed 25 January 2024].

[5] Bible Hub, 2024. *Topical Encyclopaedia: Parbar.* [Online] Available at: https://biblehub.com/topical/p/parbar.htm [Accessed 25 January 2024].

Wesley's Notes[6] and Matthew Henry's Commentary[7] both emphasise that this gate symbolised not only physical cleansing but also spiritual strength and vigilance. The guards stationed there ensured that the temple remained undefiled, reflecting the importance of guarding one's heart against corruption.

Theologically, the temple gates represent access to God's presence. The intentional organisation and assignment of gatekeepers highlight the holiness and reverence required when approaching the presence of God. The Gate of Shallecheth, as a point of transition from the secular to the sacred, symbolised the need for purity, preparation, and a heart ready to worship.

Royal Egress

Situated by the "causeway of the going up," the gate likely connected Mount Zion to Mount Moriah, serving as an elevated path for access to the temple (2 Chronicles 9:4). It has been suggested that this elevated path may have provided a direct route between the royal palace and the temple[8]. Jehoiada also stationed guards there during the coronation of King Joash (2 Kings 11:6; 2 Chronicles 23:5).

This dual function—as a point of royal procession and as a gateway to worship—underscores its symbolism as a place where earthly authority met divine presence, reminding us that the King had special access to the place of worship.

---

[6] Wesley's Notes, 2024. *Wesley's Notes.* [Online] Available at: https://biblehub.com/commentaries/wes/1_chronicles/26.htm [Accessed 25 January 2024].

[7] Matthew Henry's Commentary, 2024. *Matthew Henry's Commentary – Verses 1–19.* [Online] Available at: https://www.biblegateway.com/resources/matthew-henry/1Chr.26.1-1Chr.26.19 [Accessed 25 January 2024].

[8] Barry, J. e. a., 2016. *The Lexham Bible Dictionary: Foundation Gate.* Bellingham, WA: Lexham Press.

In reflecting on Christ as King, Jesus' kingship is described as one that surpasses all earthly power[9]. Christ reigns over the hearts and wills of humanity through His perfect obedience to God, His boundless grace, and his unfathomable love (Ephesians 3:19). Jesus Himself affirmed His kingship before Pilate, declaring, *"My kingdom is not of this world"* (John 18:36).

Unlike earthly kings, Christ's throne is not confined to a palace or temple. Instead, His rightful place is in the hearts of those who worship Him in spirit and truth. As the King of kings, He commands us to submit our lives to His authority, allowing Him to reign in every aspect of our being.

When Christ sits enthroned in our hearts, He transforms us into vessels of His love, grace, and mercy, making our lives a living testament to the light of His glory. His eternal light transforms us, radiating His divine glory through every aspect of our being. As John 1:1-13 reveals, the light of Christ is inseparable from His life, and His life carries the eternal nature, power, and deity of God. By believing in His name, we become children of God, born not of the flesh but of the will of God, and His light—unchanging, unquenchable, and eternal—dwells within us. This light bears the fullness of the Trinity, illuminating us with the power of Jehovah, Jesus, and the Holy Spirit[10].

It shines with the same radiance described in Revelation 21, where the Bride of Christ, the church, reflects the glory of God like the rarest jewels and purest gold, radiant with holiness and divine beauty. This light in us testifies to God's unshakable truth, divine perfection, and eternal presence, making our hearts the very temple where Christ reigns. As we walk in this light, we carry His glory to the nations, inviting the world into the brilliance of His peace, love, and eternal communion. Truly, the light of Christ within us is a glorious beacon of His sovereignty and grace.

---

[9] XI, P. P., 1925. *Quas Primas.* Vatican City: Libreria Editrice Vaticana.

[10] Celestin, D., 2025. Sermon: *The Light of Christ in the Church.* London: s.n.

Spiritual Deliverance & Protection

In Exodus 10:19 our attention is drawn to another reference to the west. A west wind sent by God swept the locusts into the Red Sea, leaving no trace of them behind. This act of deliverance mirrors God's ability to drive out every tormenting force, whether physical or spiritual. Similarly, Numbers 2:18-24 associates the west side with the camp of Ephraim, representing strength and protection.

The imagery consistently connects the west with cleansing, holiness, reverence, physical and spiritual deliverance, safeguarding, restoration, and the assurance of God's protection and power.

So, what can we learn about the above scriptures and their relevance to our lives today? There are three keys for us to consider about the purpose and power of prayer:

Three Principles of the West Gate

1. Purify the Temple of Our Hearts

Don't let sin or distractions accumulate in your life. Purify your heart to become a suitable vessel for His presence. Confess sin, forsake addictions, let go of idols, and seek God's forgiveness. Remove anything in your life that blocks God's work.

2. Seeking the Revelation of Christ's Glory

Recognise the sovereign and majestical right of Jesus to sit enthroned in our hearts and ruling every area of our lives. Like the priests who ministered near the Holy of Holies, approach God with reverence and expectancy. Resetting our vision of who Christ is, rightly seeing Him as He deserves and enjoying that forever.

3. Renewal and Revival

True revival is the sovereign work of God whereby he renews his people individually and corporately by the Holy Spirit, affecting both quality of faith, behaviour and life. Witnessing yourself transform into who Christ is from day to day; To see our lives return to spiritual usefulness and activity, i.e.:

- Cultivating a lifestyle of prayer.

- Deepening your understanding of Scripture.

- Uniting with the church in prayer and fellowship.

- Bearing witness to God's work in your life.

- Impacting your community and the world with the light of Jesus Christ.

This book aims to facilitate your journey of intercession, transformation, and hope. Embrace this opportunity to draw closer to God, and watch as He moves in powerful ways. Whether you actively participated in the 100 days of prayer season, in any way, or wish to kick-start or supercharge your prayer life again to continue enjoying God through prayer, this book serves you as a guideline. Many experienced breakthroughs in their lives as a result of joining the prayer calls and encountering God.

Can this work for you, too? Yes, by the will of God!

Encouraging the Heart

At both the beginning and end of the 100 Days of Prayer, group members were invited to reflect on their spiritual journey through a series of survey questions, which centred around the three principles of the west gate. The results reveal profound spiritual growth and a renewed hunger for God's presence.

Purify the Temple of Our Hearts

One of the primary goals of the 100 Days of Prayer was to encourage participants to pursue spiritual purity and holiness.

When asked, "On a scale of 1 to 10, how would you now describe the state of your heart in relation to spiritual purity?"

- Before: Only 2% scored a 10. After: 35% scored a 10.

- This marks an 18-fold increase in hunger for holiness!

When asked, "Do you currently feel any burdens, sins, or distractions that are preventing you from fully experiencing God's presence?"

- Before: 81% admitted to carrying such burdens. After: 100% reported experiencing breakthrough, with hearts freed from distractions.

When asked, "How often do you intentionally reflect on the condition of your heart before God?"

- Before: 65% reflected daily. After: 82% now engage in daily heart reflection.

When asked, "In the past month, how often have you sought to encounter Christ more deeply through prayer or scripture?"

- Before: 49% pursued this daily. After: 59% now intentionally seek deeper encounters with Christ daily.

When asked, "Are there areas in your life where you desire a greater revelation of Christ?"

- Before: 92% expressed a strong desire. After: 100% experienced a greater revelation of Christ's glory!

Seeking the Revelation of Christ's Glory

The theme of seeking God's glory was central to this journey, and the survey highlights the profound transformation participants experienced.

When asked, "How would you rate your understanding and personal experience of Christ's glory on a scale of 1 to 10?"

- Before: 7% rated it a 10. After: 35% rated it a 10.

- This represents a 5-fold increase in experiencing Christ's glory!

"How often do you pray specifically for renewal or revival in your life or others' lives?"

- Before: 70% prayed for this daily or weekly, with 47% praying daily. After: 82% now pray for renewal or revival daily or weekly, with 65% committing to daily prayer.

Renewal and Revival

Participants were also asked about their spiritual vitality—their sense of being alive in their faith and excited about God's work.

When asked, "On a scale of 1 to 10, how would you rate your spiritual vitality at this moment?"

- Before: Only 9% rated it a 10. After: 29% rated it a 10.

- This represents a 3-fold increase in spiritual vitality!

Other Thanksgivings

The 100 Days of Prayer produced remarkable growth across several additional areas of spiritual life:

"How would you rate your understanding of Scripture on a scale of 1 to 10?"

- Before: 5% rated their understanding as a 10. After: 24% rated it a 10.

- This reflects a 5-fold increase in engagement with God's Word!

"How often do you engage in personal prayer time?"

- Before: 74% prayed daily. After: 94% now commit to daily prayer.

"How connected do you feel to UK PCEA in terms of prayer support?"

- Before: 44% felt very connected. After: 82% now feel very connected. This shows a doubled sense of connection within the body of Christ.

These statistics are a testament to the profound work God accomplished in the lives of the group members during the 100 Days of Prayer. Hearts were purified, faith was renewed, and the presence of Christ became more tangible than ever before. This can be your testimony and song too, if you make a decision today to pray.

Throughout this prayer journey, every 10 days, you will read real-life testimonies from people who have experienced God's power and work in their lives, offering encouragement to your heart. It's essential to remember that your journey to answered prayer is personal—between you, God, and His promises—fulfilled through faith in Jesus, in whom all God's promises are *yes* and *amen*.

The timing of answered prayer is entirely in God's sovereign hands. However, the *waiting period* can be challenging, especially when answers do not come as quickly as we hope but keep on trusting God for He knows what you need.

Hebrews 11, the *chapter of faith*, reminds us of the many saints who believed and walked with God daily, living a life of faith and expectancy. Their faith was credited to them as righteousness—yet many did not see the fulfilment of the promises in their lifetime. These faithful ones now serve as a *great cloud of witnesses* for us, cheering us on as we continue the Christian race. God saw it fit that their testimonies should strengthen and inspire our faith today.

So, to keep the flame of faith burning, let the stories of those—ancient and modern—who have praised God for answered prayers or for answers still on the way encourage you. If God did it for them, He can do it for you as well.

Getting Started

So, you sense your faith level rising to start your prayer journey but you feel your "flesh" resist you. Prayer can sometimes feel challenging to get started. There are times in our Christian walk where we experience spiritual exhaustion and weakness[11]; Your faith level is low and weary from the passive or active persecution of the world and its cares. We may find ourselves struggling to focus during prayer, running out of words, or drifting toward prayers that may not align with God's will—even struggling finding the motivation to pray. I think all Christians have experienced this at some point in their faith journey.

However, I've found that using Scripture as a guide transforms prayer into powerful and focused experiences. When we pray with Scripture, we align our hearts with the revealed will of God and away from our own efforts to find words. His Word provides both the inspiration and the structure to help us pray with clarity, purpose, and confidence before the throne of grace. Indeed the Holy Spirit helps us in our weaknesses by praying for us, strengthening us, and healing our wounds as described in Romans 8:26-28.

Why Pray with Scripture?

Scripture is God's Word—His revealed will for His people. By praying Scripture, we stay rooted in God's truth, ensuring our prayers align with His purposes and promises; It sharpens our focus and helps us avoid personal distractions; We allow God to shape our desires, emotions, and petitions to reflect His will.

---

[11] MacArthur, J., 1998. *Bearing Up the Weak in Prayer.* [Online] Available at: https://www.gty.org/library/sermons-library/90-202/bearing-up-the-weak-in-prayer [Accessed 15 Feb 2025].

As you approach prayer through Scripture, understanding the text is key. Begin by identifying the main meaning of the passage—exegetically, what is God saying here so I can mould my understanding to His revealed will? When we grasp the essence of the text in our hearts, we can, through the Holy Spirit's help, transform it into prayers that flow from the heart saturated with God's will.

When the Word of God dwells in us richly, it naturally shapes our prayers, aligning them with His will and purposes. As Colossians 3:16 encourages, *"Let the word of Christ dwell in you richly, teaching and admonishing one another in all wisdom, singing psalms and hymns and spiritual songs, with thankfulness in your hearts to God."*

When God's Word takes root in our hearts, it flows out in beautiful and transformative ways—whether through teaching, singing, or heartfelt gratitude[12]. This richness in Scripture enables us to pray with a depth that is saturated with His truth, producing prayers that glorify Him and resonate with His will.

The Scriptures serve as a guide for our prayers by revealing different aspects of our relationship with God. They may reveal something about God, Christ, or the Holy Spirit, prompting us to praise Him. They may recount what God has done, leading us to thank Him and trust in His works. They may show us what God expects of us, compelling us to cry out for His help. Or, they may highlight areas where we have fallen short, inviting us to confess our sins.

Essentially, all of Scripture can lead us into one or more of these responses: praise, thanksgiving, a plea for help, or confession—drawing us closer to God in every moment of prayer.

---

[12] Platt, D., 2017. *Let the Word Dwell in You Richly (Colossians 3:16)*. [Online] Available at: https://radical.net/podcasts/pray-the-word/let-the-word-dwell-in-you-richly-colossians-316/ [Accessed 27 January 2025].

Steps to Pray the Scriptures

John Piper has suggested a very useful tool in aiding Christians to pray, called the IOUS prayer acronym[13]. Inspired from the Psalms, it provides a helpful framework for praying Scripture:

1. **Inclination**: Pray for a heart inclined toward God and His Word. *"Incline my heart to your testimonies, and not to selfish gain!"* (Psalm 119:36)

2. **Open Eyes**: Pray for open eyes to see the wonders of God's Word. *"Open my eyes, that I may behold wondrous things out of your law."* (Psalm 119:18). Reflect on what the passage reveals about God, His character, His promises, or His instructions.

3. **Unity of Heart**: Pray for a united heart that fears and reveres God. *"Teach me your way, O LORD, that I may walk in your truth; unite my heart to fear your name."* (Psalm 86:11)

4. **Satisfaction**: Pray for satisfaction in God and His steadfast love. *"Satisfy us in the morning with your steadfast love, that we may rejoice and be glad all our days."* (Psalm 90:14)

For example: When praying with Psalm 23, *"The LORD is my shepherd; I shall not want,"* your prayer might look like this:

Inclination: "Lord, incline my heart to trust You as my Shepherd, instead of seeking security in worldly things."

Open Eyes: "Open my eyes to see how You provide for me daily and guide me in ways I may not even notice."

---

[13] Piper, J., 2017. *How Do I Pray the Bible?*. [Online] Available at: https://www.desiringgod.org/interviews/how-do-i-pray-the-bible [Accessed 26 January 2025].

Unity of Heart: "Unite my heart to follow You as my Shepherd, trusting Your leading above all else."

Satisfaction: "Satisfy me with the truth that You are enough, and I shall not want for anything outside of You."

When you pray with Scripture, you are allowing God's Word to shape your thoughts, align your desires with His will, and deepen your connection to Him. Let the Scriptures anchor your prayers, and you will discover a profound richness and clarity in your time with the Lord.

The rest of this book will be a series of daily guides, based on the 30-minute structure of the prayer calls, to assist you in your ongoing prayer journey. We pray that you experience a revival in your prayer life and a renewed sense of the Lord's presence, in Jesus' name.

100 Day Prayer Journal

Day 1: Scriptural Foundation of Prayer – Why Pray?

1. **Opening Worship**

   - Begin your time by praising God for His faithfulness and His invitation to pray. Reflect on the truth of John 15:7 and thank God for the privilege of abiding in Him.

2. **Scripture Meditation**

   - Read and meditate on Matthew 7:7. Reflect on what it means to actively ask, seek, and knock. Write down how this verse inspires you to persist in prayer.

3. **Personal Prayers**

   - **Confession:** Ask God to reveal any areas where you may not be abiding in Him or seeking Him with pure motives (James 4:3). Confess these areas and ask for His cleansing.

   - **Petitions:** Pray for a deeper desire to know God's Word, that it would abide in your heart and guide your prayers.

4. **Intercession**

   - Pray for your church, your family, and your community, asking that they also experience the joy of abiding in Christ and the power of prayer. Use John 15:7 to guide your intercessions.

5. **Closing Prayer and Thanksgiving**

   - Thank God for the confidence we have in prayer and His promise to respond to His children. Ask for a continued hunger to seek Him daily, ending with a prayer of surrender to His will.

Daily Reflections and Insights

Today's Reflection:
What did God reveal to you about prayer and His will through today's scriptures?

Prayer Insight:
What specific burdens or needs did you bring before God today? How did you experience His presence in your prayer time?

Gratitude Journal:
List three things you are thankful for as you prayed today:

1.

2.

3.

Day 2: Confidence in Prayer

1. **Opening Worship**

   - Begin by praising God for being approachable and for hearing our prayers.

   - Sing or reflect on a hymn that speaks of God's faithfulness and love, like "What a Friend We Have in Jesus."

   - Acknowledge God as the sovereign ruler who invites us to draw near to Him.

2. **Scripture Meditation**

   - Read and meditate on 1 John 5:14–16 and reflect on what it means to pray confidently, trusting that God hears prayers aligned with His will.

3. **Personal Prayers**

   - Ask God to help you approach Him with faith and humility and confess any fears, doubts, or hesitations in your prayer life.

   - Pray for a heart aligned with God's will and the ability to discern His purposes as you pray.

4. **Intercession**

   - Pray for the Church to remain faithful in prayer, confident in God's promises.

   - Intercede for friends, family, or others in need of God's intervention and comfort.

   - Pray for your enemies or those you find difficult to love (Matthew 5:44).

5. **Closing Prayer and Thanksgiving**

- Thank God for the gift of prayer and the assurance that He hears and answers according to His will.

- Close with a song of thanksgiving or a declaration of faith.

Daily Reflections and Insights

Today's Reflection:
What did God reveal to you about prayer and His will through today's scriptures?

Prayer Insight:
What specific burdens or needs did you bring before God today? How did you experience His presence in your prayer time?

Gratitude Journal:
List three things you are thankful for as you prayed today:

1.

2.

3.

Day 3: The Supremacy of God

1. **Opening Worship**

   - Begin with reverent worship, acknowledging God as supreme over all creation.

   - Praise Him for His greatness, declaring, *"Our God is in the heavens; he does all that he pleases"* (Psalm 115:3).

   - Sing or reflect on a hymn such as "How Great Thou Art" or "All Hail the Power of Jesus' Name."

2. **Scripture Meditation**

   - Read and meditate on Colossians 1:16: "For by him all things were created, in heaven and on earth, visible and invisible, whether thrones or dominions or rulers or authorities—all things were created through him and for him."

   - Reflect on how God's supremacy is revealed in the vastness of creation and in His ultimate purpose for all things.

   - Ask God to open your eyes to His glory and majesty as you meditate.

3. **Personal Prayers**

   - Acknowledge God's sovereignty in your life and surrender your plans to Him.

   - Pray for greater awe and understanding of His supremacy.

   - Confess areas where you have doubted or failed to honour God's ultimate authority.

4. **Intercession**

- Pray for the Church to fully grasp the majesty and sovereignty of God.

- Lift up leaders and nations, asking for God's will to be done in the affairs of the world.

- Pray for those who do not yet recognise God's supremacy, that their hearts may be turned to Him.

5. **Closing Prayer and Thanksgiving**

- Thank God for being the creator and sustainer of all things, and for including you in His eternal plan.

- Declare your trust in His wisdom and ways, as Romans 11:33 reminds us: "Oh, the depth of the riches and wisdom and knowledge of God! How unsearchable are his judgments and how inscrutable his ways!"

- End with a song of praise or a moment of silent adoration.

Daily Reflections and Insights

Today's Reflection:
What did God reveal to you about His sovereignty and supremacy through today's scriptures?

Prayer Insight:
How does knowing God's supreme authority bring peace or clarity to your current circumstances?

Gratitude Journal:
List something you are thankful for as you reflect on God's supremacy today:

Day 4: The Positional Advantage of Being with Christ

1. **Opening Worship**

   - Begin by worshipping God for the new identity and purpose He gives us in Christ.

   - Sing or reflect on the words of *"In Christ Alone"* or *"Amazing Grace."*

   - Declare 2 Corinthians 5:17: "Therefore, if anyone is in Christ, he is a new creation. The old has passed away; behold, the new has come."

2. **Scripture Meditation**

   - Read and meditate on Galatians 2:20: "I have been crucified with Christ. It is no longer I who live, but Christ who lives in me. And the life I now live in the flesh I live by faith in the Son of God, who loved me and gave himself for me."

   - Reflect on the truth that your life is now hidden in Christ, and consider how this impacts your daily walk with Him.

   - Ask the Holy Spirit to reveal areas where you need to fully embrace your position in Christ.

3. **Personal Prayers**

   - Thank God for making you a new creation in Christ.

   - Pray for the strength to live in the reality of being crucified with Christ.

   - Confess any areas where you have been holding on to the "old self" and ask God to help you walk in your new identity.

4. Intercession

- Pray for others who may be struggling to understand or accept their identity in Christ.

- Ask God to help the Church live out its calling as a "chosen race, a royal priesthood, a holy nation" (1 Peter 2:9).

- Intercede for those who are still searching for purpose, that they may find it in Christ.

5. Closing Prayer and Thanksgiving

- End with thanksgiving for the privilege of being with Christ and the transformation it brings.

- Speak aloud, 1 Peter 2:9: "But you are a chosen race, a royal priesthood, a holy nation, a people for his own possession, that you may proclaim the excellencies of him who called you out of darkness into his marvellous light."

- Close with a prayer of commitment to live boldly as a reflection of Christ.

Daily Reflections and Insights

Today's Reflection:
How has the reality of being a "new creation" in Christ changed your outlook on life?

Prayer Insight:
What steps can you take to live fully in the positional advantage of being with Christ?

Gratitude Journal:

List three things you are thankful for as you reflected on your position in Christ today:

1.

2.

3.

Day 5: The Positional Advantage of Being Filled with the Holy Spirit

1. **Opening Worship**

   - Begin by praising God for the gift of the Holy Spirit, who empowers, guides, and comforts us.

   - Reflect on Luke 3:22: "And the Holy Spirit descended on him in bodily form, like a dove; and a voice came from heaven, 'You are my beloved Son; with you I am well pleased.'"

   - Worship with songs like "Holy Spirit, You Are Welcome Here" or "Spirit of the Living God."

2. **Scripture Meditation**

   - Meditate on Romans 15:13: "May the God of hope fill you with all joy and peace in believing, so that by the power of the Holy Spirit you may abound in hope."

   - Reflect on how the Holy Spirit enables you to experience joy, peace, and hope in your life.

   - Ask the Spirit to reveal His active presence in areas of your life where you need His strength and guidance.

3. **Personal Prayers**

   - Thank God for making your body a temple of the Holy Spirit (1 Corinthians 6:19).

   - Surrender areas of your life where you need the Holy Spirit's power and leadership.

   - Pray for a fresh filling of the Spirit, asking for renewed strength, wisdom, and discernment in your daily walk.

4. **Intercession**

- Pray for the Church to be filled with the Holy Spirit, walking in His power and unity.

- Intercede for believers struggling to experience the fullness of the Spirit in their lives.

- Lift up those who have not yet encountered the Holy Spirit, asking that they be drawn to Christ and receive the Spirit's transformative work.

5. **Closing Prayer and Thanksgiving**

- Thank God for the abundant hope and peace that come through the power of the Holy Spirit.

- Declare Romans 15:13 over your life and others, committing to live in step with the Spirit daily.

- End by asking for the Spirit's continual guidance and presence throughout the day.

Daily Reflections and Insights

Today's Reflection:
How have you experienced the joy, peace, and hope that come from being filled with the Holy Spirit?

Prayer Insight:
In what ways can you rely more on the Holy Spirit's power and guidance in your daily life?

Gratitude Journal:
List the ways the Holy Spirit has worked in your life recently:

Day 6: Seeking the Blood of Jesus Christ

1. **Opening Worship**

   - Thank God for the cleansing and redemptive power of Jesus' blood.

   - Sing a song that magnifies the blood of Jesus, such as "There is Power in the Blood" or "Nothing But the Blood of Jesus."

2. **Scripture Meditation**

   - Read 1 John 1:7 and thank God for the fellowship and cleansing that comes through Christ's blood.

   - Read Matthew 26:27-28 and reflect on the significance of Jesus' sacrifice for the forgiveness of sins.

   - Read Acts 20:28 and acknowledge how Christ's blood secures His people and His Church.

3. **Personal Prayers**

   - Confess any sins, knowing that Jesus' blood cleanses and restores you.

   - Ask God to deepen your understanding of Christ's sacrifice and its impact on your life.

   - Pray for a fresh revelation of the power of Jesus' blood in your spiritual walk.

4. **Intercession**

   - Pray for your family and loved ones, asking God to cover them with the blood of Jesus.

   - Lift up your church and spiritual leaders, asking for protection and cleansing through Christ's blood.

- Intercede for those who have not yet accepted Jesus, that they may come to understand His redemptive work.

5. **Closing Prayer and Commitment**

- Thank Jesus for His blood, which has redeemed, cleansed, and sealed you in His covenant.

- Commit to walking in the light, living a life that honours His sacrifice.

Daily Reflections and Insights

Today's Reflection:
How has the blood of Jesus impacted your life?

Prayer Insight:
What specific area in your life do you need Jesus' cleansing power the most?

Commitment Journal:

Write three ways you will walk in the power of Jesus' blood today:

1.

2.

3.

Day 7: Seeking Holiness

1. **Opening Worship**

   - Praise God for His holiness and His call for us to be holy.

   - Sing a song of dedication, such as "Holiness (Take My Life)" or "Refiner's Fire."

2. **Scripture Meditation**

   - Read Hebrews 12:14 and pray for the grace to pursue holiness in all areas of life.

   - Read Romans 6:22 and thank God for setting you free from sin so you may live in righteousness.

   - Read Hebrews 12:10 and reflect on how God's discipline helps shape you into His holiness.

3. **Personal Prayers**

   - Confess any sin or impurity, asking God to cleanse your heart and mind.

   - Ask God for strength to resist temptation and live in obedience to His Word.

   - Pray for a deep desire to walk in holiness daily.

4. **Intercession**

   - Pray for your family and loved ones to grow in holiness and righteousness.

   - Lift up your church, asking God to sanctify the body of Christ.

   - Intercede for believers struggling with sin, asking God to lead them into purity and freedom.

5. Closing Prayer and Commitment

- Thank God for His grace that enables you to live a holy life.

- Commit to pursuing holiness and reflecting Christ's character in all you do.

Daily Reflections and Insights

Today's Reflection:
What steps can you take to pursue holiness more intentionally?

Prayer Insight:
In what area of your life do you need God's refining work the most?

Commitment Journal:
Write three ways you will pursue holiness today:

1.

2.

3.

Day 8: A Heart of Repentance

1. **Opening Worship**

   - Acknowledge God's holiness and the call to repentance.

   - Sing a song such as "Lord, I Need You" or "Create in Me a Clean Heart."

2. **Scripture Meditation**

   - Read Isaiah 30:15 and reflect on how repentance and rest lead to salvation.

   - Read Luke 5:31-32 and consider Jesus' call for sinners to turn back to God.

   - Read Acts 3:19 and meditate on the promise of spiritual renewal through repentance.

3. **Personal Prayers**

   - Confess your sins before God and seek His forgiveness.

   - Ask God to give you a truly repentant heart that turns away from sin.

   - Pray for strength to walk in obedience and live a transformed life.

4. **Intercession**

   - Pray for loved ones who need to experience true repentance.

   - Ask God to stir the hearts of His Church toward repentance and revival.

   - Intercede for your nation, seeking God's mercy and a turning back to Him.

5. Closing Prayer and Commitment

- Thank God for His mercy and the cleansing power of repentance.

- Commit to living a life of continual repentance and renewal in Christ.

Daily Reflections and Insights

Today's Reflection:
What is God revealing to you about the importance of repentance?

Prayer Insight:
Is there anything specific in your life that God is calling you to turn away from?

Commitment Journal:
Write three ways you will walk in repentance today:

1.

2.

3.

Day 9: The Tongue/Words

1. **Opening Worship**

   - Thank God for the gift of speech and the power of words.

   - Sing a song such as "Let the Words of My Mouth" or "I Surrender."

2. **Scripture Meditation**

   - Read 1 Peter 3:10 and reflect on the connection between words and a blessed life.

   - Read Colossians 4:6 and meditate on how your speech can be filled with grace.

   - Read Ephesians 4:29 and consider how your words can build others up.

3. **Personal Prayers**

   - Ask God to help you control your tongue and speak words that honour Him.

   - Confess any past words that may have hurt others and seek forgiveness.

   - Pray for wisdom to speak life-giving words in every situation.

4. **Intercession**

   - Pray for your family and friends, that their words may reflect God's grace.

   - Ask God to purify the speech of leaders, teachers, and those with influence.

- Intercede for those struggling with gossip, lying, or hurtful speech.

5. **Closing Prayer and Commitment**

- Thank God for the ability to use words to glorify Him and edify others.

- Commit to speaking words that reflect the love, truth, and wisdom of God.

Daily Reflections and Insights

Today's Reflection:
How can your words reflect God's grace more effectively?

Prayer Insight:
Is there a specific area in your speech where you need God's help?

Commitment Journal:
Write three ways you will use your words to glorify God today:

1.

2.

3.

Day 10: Clean and Pure Heart

1. **Opening Worship**

   - Praise God for His power to cleanse and renew your heart.

   - Sing a worship song such as "Purify My Heart" or "Create in Me a Clean Heart."

2. **Scripture Meditation**

   - Read Matthew 6:21 and reflect on where your heart's treasure truly is.

   - Read Proverbs 3:5 and meditate on trusting God fully with your heart.

   - Read Proverbs 4:23 and consider how guarding your heart affects your actions.

3. **Personal Prayers**

   - Ask God to purify your heart from anything that does not align with His will.

   - Confess any areas where your heart has been divided or impure.

   - Pray for a heart that fully trusts and follows God's guidance.

4. **Intercession**

   - Pray for your loved ones to develop hearts that are pure and devoted to God.

   - Ask God to give church leaders and believers integrity and sincerity of heart.

- Intercede for those struggling with bitterness, unforgiveness, or impure desires.

5. **Closing Prayer and Commitment**

   - Thank God for His transforming work in your heart.

   - Commit to guarding your heart and filling it with His truth and righteousness.

Daily Reflections and Insights

Today's Reflection:
What influences are shaping your heart today?

Prayer Insight:
Are there any areas where you need to surrender your heart fully to God?

Commitment Journal:
Write three ways you will cultivate a clean and pure heart today:

1.

2.

3.

"I experienced a spiritual awakening during the 100 Days of Prayer, and my zeal for God has been reignited. I have become more aware of the urgency to call on God over my circumstances, more than ever before. When I first gave my life to Christ, I had a deep love for Him, but over the years, I noticed that love and trust were declining. During this time of prayer, I felt that fire for God being rekindled, and I pray it will continue to burn. My desire is for my love for God to grow deeper than it has ever been."

Lessons in Prayer

The Purpose of Prayer is Transformation

Prayer is not just about asking and receiving. It is about transformation.

Jesus calls us to ask, seek, and knock (Matthew 7:7), but the deeper meaning goes beyond material requests. Prayer reshapes our hearts, aligns our desires with God's will, and helps us overcome the nature of sin.

When we pray, we invite the Holy Spirit to work within us. This exchange changes our perceptions, thoughts, and convictions. The more we pray, the more God's word takes root in us. As His word becomes alive in our hearts, we see His promises fulfilled in our lives.

Prayers filled with emotion can touch God's heart, but what truly moves His hand is alignment with His word. A transformed heart has a greater capacity for answered prayer

Day 11: Thought Life

1. **Opening Worship**

   - Praise God for the power to renew your mind and transform your thoughts.

   - Sing a worship song such as "Renew My Mind" or "Lord, I Offer My Life to You."

2. **Scripture Meditation**

   - Read Romans 12:2 and ask God to renew your mind according to His will.

   - Read Philippians 4:8 and meditate on filling your thoughts with what is true, noble, and pure.

   - Read 2 Timothy 1:7 and reflect on how God has given you a spirit of power, love, and self-discipline.

3. **Personal Prayers**

   - Ask God to purify your thought life and remove any negative or sinful patterns.

   - Pray for the discipline to focus on thoughts that align with His Word.

   - Confess any struggles with anxious, impure, or destructive thoughts.

4. **Intercession**

   - Pray for family and friends to experience the renewal of their minds.

   - Ask God to help believers develop minds that are filled with His wisdom and truth.

- Intercede for those battling fear, anxiety, or mental strongholds.

5. Closing Prayer and Commitment

- Thank God for His Spirit, which gives you power, love, and self-discipline.

- Commit to guarding your thoughts and filling your mind with His truth.

Daily Reflections and Insights

Today's Reflection:
What thoughts have been shaping your actions and attitudes lately?

Prayer Insight:
Are there any thought patterns you need to surrender to God today?

Commitment Journal:
Write three ways you will cultivate a renewed mind today:

1.

2.

3.

Day 12: Mindset

1. Opening Worship

- Praise God for giving you the ability to have the mind of Christ.

- Sing a worship song such as "Lord, Transform Me" or "Be Thou My Vision."

2. Scripture Meditation

- Read Philippians 4:7 and thank God for His peace that guards your heart and mind.

- Read Romans 12:2 and reflect on the importance of renewing your mind in alignment with God's will.

- Read 1 Corinthians 2:16 and meditate on the truth that you have the mind of Christ.

3. Personal Prayers

- Ask God to help you reject worldly thinking and embrace His perspective.

- Pray for a mindset that aligns with His truth, wisdom, and purpose.

- Surrender any thoughts, attitudes, or beliefs that hinder spiritual growth.

4. Intercession

- Pray for your family and loved ones to develop a Christ-centred mindset.

- Lift up church leaders and believers, asking God to renew their minds daily.

- Intercede for those who struggle with negative, anxious, or self-defeating thoughts.

5. Closing Prayer and Commitment

- Thank God for the transformation He is bringing to your mind and thoughts.

- Commit to daily renewing your mind in His Word and walking in His wisdom.

Daily Reflections and Insights

Today's Reflection:
How does your current mindset align with the truth of God's Word?

Prayer Insight:
What areas of your mindset need to be transformed by God today?

Commitment Journal:
Write three ways you will cultivate a Christ-centred mindset today:

1.

2.

3.

Day 13: Soulset

1. **Opening Worship**

   - Praise God for being the keeper and sanctifier of your soul.

   - Sing a worship song such as "Refiner's Fire" or "Purify My Heart."

2. **Scripture Meditation**

   - Read 1 Thessalonians 5:23 and thank God for His sanctifying work in your spirit, soul, and body.

   - Read Ephesians 6:12 and acknowledge the spiritual battle over your soul, asking for divine strength.

   - Read Matthew 16:26 and reflect on the value of your soul in light of eternity.

3. **Personal Prayers**

   - Ask God to purify your soul and align your desires with His will.

   - Pray for discernment to guard your soul against worldly distractions and temptations.

   - Surrender any burdens, sins, or attachments that hinder spiritual growth.

4. **Intercession**

   - Pray for your family and loved ones to prioritise their souls and seek God above all else.

   - Lift up those struggling spiritually, asking God to draw them back to Him.

- Intercede for the Church to be strengthened in soul and spirit against spiritual warfare.

5. **Closing Prayer and Commitment**

   - Thank God for His peace and protection over your soul.

   - Commit to nurturing your soul daily through prayer, scripture, and worship.

Daily Reflections and Insights

Today's Reflection:
How can you prioritise the health of your soul in your daily life?

Prayer Insight:
What worldly distractions do you need to let go of to focus on your soul's well-being?

Commitment Journal:
Write three ways you will guard and strengthen your soul today:

1.

2.

3.

Day 14: Your Heart

1. **Opening Worship**

    *   Praise God for His ability to transform and guide your heart.

    *   Sing a worship song such as "Change My Heart, Oh God" or "Purify My Heart."

2. **Scripture Meditation**

    *   Read Matthew 6:21 and reflect on where your true treasure lies.

    *   Read Proverbs 3:5 and surrender your heart fully to God's wisdom and guidance.

    *   Read Proverbs 4:23 and ask God to help you guard your heart from negative influences.

3. **Personal Prayers**

    *   Ask God to realign your heart's desires with His will.

    *   Pray for wisdom and discernment to keep your heart pure and focused on Him.

    *   Surrender any bitterness, unforgiveness, or distractions that hinder your heart's devotion to God.

4. **Intercession**

    *   Pray for family and friends to develop hearts that trust in God completely.

    *   Lift up those who are struggling with heartache, asking God to bring healing and peace.

- Intercede for the Church, that believers would have hearts fully committed to Christ.

5. **Closing Prayer and Commitment**

- Thank God for His faithfulness in shaping your heart according to His purpose.

- Commit to guarding your heart and keeping it focused on Him.

Daily Reflections and Insights

Today's Reflection:
What is your heart most drawn to, and does it align with God's will?

Prayer Insight:
In what area of your life do you need to trust God with all your heart?

Commitment Journal:
Write three ways you will guard and align your heart with God today:

1.

2.

3.

Day 15: The Ears

1. **Opening Worship**

   • Praise God for the ability to hear His voice and receive His wisdom.

   • Sing a worship song such as "Speak, O Lord" or "Open the Eyes of My Heart."

2. **Scripture Meditation**

   • Read Matthew 13:9, 13-16 and reflect on the importance of having ears that truly hear and understand God's word.

   • Read Proverbs 22:17-21 and ask God for wisdom to discern and apply His truth.

   • Read Romans 10:17 and pray for a heart that grows in faith through hearing the Word of Christ.

3. **Personal Prayers**

   • Ask God to open your ears to His voice and silence distractions that hinder your spiritual hearing.

   • Pray for discernment to recognise truth and reject deception.

   • Repent for times you have ignored God's guidance and ask for renewed sensitivity to His Word.

4. **Intercession**

   • Pray for family and friends to have ears that hear God's truth and walk in obedience.

   • Lift up church leaders and teachers, asking God to anoint their words so others may hear and grow in faith.

- Intercede for those who struggle to hear God, that He may reveal Himself to them clearly.

5. **Closing Prayer and Commitment**

- Thank God for speaking to you through His Word and His Spirit.

- Commit to being intentional about listening to God and obeying what He reveals.

Daily Reflections and Insights

Today's Reflection:
How well do you listen when God speaks, and what distractions do you need to remove?

Prayer Insight:
What is God speaking to you about in this season, and how can you respond?

Commitment Journal:
Write three ways you will be intentional about listening to God today:

1.

2.

3.

Day 16: Spiritual Eyesight

1. **Opening Worship**

   - Praise God for being the light that guides and reveals truth.

   - Sing a worship song such as "Open the Eyes of My Heart" or "Be Thou My Vision."

2. **Scripture Meditation**

   - Read 1 John 2:16 and reflect on how the lust of the eyes can lead us away from God.

   - Read Acts 9:18 and ask God to remove any spiritual blindness that may be hindering your walk with Him.

   - Read Matthew 6:22 and pray for spiritual eyes that see clearly and bring light to your soul.

3. **Personal Prayers**

   - Ask God to give you discernment to see things through His perspective rather than the world's.

   - Pray against any form of spiritual blindness or deception in your life.

   - Seek God's help in guarding your eyes from distractions and temptations that lead you away from Him.

4. **Intercession**

   - Pray for loved ones who may be spiritually blind, asking God to open their eyes to His truth.

   - Lift up church leaders and ministers, that they may have clear spiritual vision to lead others wisely.

- Intercede for those who are struggling to see God's plan in difficult seasons, that they may receive divine clarity.

5. **Closing Prayer and Commitment**

- Thank God for being the light in your life and for opening your spiritual eyes.

- Commit to keeping your eyes fixed on Jesus and seeking His guidance in all things.

Daily Reflections and Insights

Today's Reflection:
What worldly distractions have been affecting your spiritual vision?

Prayer Insight:
What steps can you take to ensure your spiritual eyesight remains clear and focused on God?

Commitment Journal:
Write three ways you will guard and strengthen your spiritual eyesight today:

1.

2.

3.

Day 17: Repentance

1. **Opening Worship**

   - Thank God for His mercy and the gift of repentance that leads to life.

   - Sing a song of surrender such as "Lord, I Need You" or "Create in Me a Clean Heart."

2. **Scripture Meditation**

   - Read Acts 3:18-19 and reflect on how repentance brings times of refreshing from the Lord.

   - Read 2 Corinthians 7:9-10 and consider the difference between godly sorrow and worldly sorrow.

   - Read Revelation 3:3 and ask God to help you remain watchful and repentant in your walk with Him.

3. **Personal Prayers**

   - Confess any known sins and ask God for a heart of true repentance.

   - Pray for godly sorrow that leads to transformation rather than just regret.

   - Ask the Holy Spirit to reveal any areas in your life where repentance is needed.

4. **Intercession**

   - Pray for family members and friends who need to turn back to God.

   - Ask God to bring revival and repentance in your church and community.

- Intercede for nations and leaders, that they may turn to God in humility and righteousness.

5. **Closing Prayer and Commitment**

   - Thank God for His grace that forgives and restores.

   - Commit to living a life of ongoing repentance and alignment with God's will.

Daily Reflections and Insights

Today's Reflection:
What is one area in your life where God is calling you to deeper repentance?

Prayer Insight:
How does true repentance bring spiritual renewal and transformation?

Commitment Journal:
Write three ways you will walk in repentance today:

1.

2.

3.

Day 18: Pride and Ego

1. **Opening Worship**

   - Thank God for His wisdom that humbles the proud and exalts the humble.

   - Sing a song of surrender such as "Humble Thyself in the Sight of the Lord" or "I Surrender All."

2. **Scripture Meditation**

   - Read Proverbs 8:13 and reflect on God's hatred for pride and arrogance.

   - Read 1 Samuel 2:3 and consider how God weighs the deeds of the proud.

   - Read Proverbs 16:18 and meditate on the dangers of pride leading to destruction.

3. **Personal Prayers**

   - Ask God to search your heart and reveal any prideful attitudes or ego-driven actions.

   - Pray for a spirit of humility, that you may walk in God's wisdom and grace.

   - Confess any moments of arrogance and surrender your heart fully to Christ.

4. **Intercession**

   - Pray for family and friends to embrace humility and reject pride.

   - Ask God to help church leaders and believers walk in humility as they serve.

- Intercede for leaders in government, business, and communities to lead with humility rather than arrogance.

5. **Closing Prayer and Commitment**

   - Thank God for His grace that transforms pride into humility.

   - Commit to walking in humility and depending fully on God in all things.

Daily Reflections and Insights

Today's Reflection:
How has pride affected your relationship with God and others?

Prayer Insight:
In what ways can you cultivate a humble and surrendered heart before God?

Commitment Journal:
Write three ways you will practice humility today:

1.

2.

3.

Day 19: The Mind of Christ

1. Opening Worship

- Praise God for the gift of the mind of Christ, which transforms our thinking and perspectives.

- Sing a song of surrender and renewal such as "Change My Heart, O God" or "Open the Eyes of My Heart, Lord."

2. Scripture Meditation

- Read Philippians 4:7 and meditate on the peace of God that guards your heart and mind in Christ Jesus.

- Read Romans 12:2 and reflect on how God transforms your mind, enabling you to understand His will.

- Read 1 Corinthians 2:16 and thank God for the privilege of having the mind of Christ.

3. Personal Prayers

- Ask God to renew your mind and replace worldly patterns with Christ-centred thinking.

- Pray for peace that transcends understanding, to guard your heart and mind in all situations.

- Surrender any thought patterns that are not aligned with the mind of Christ.

4. Intercession

- Pray for family and loved ones to experience the renewing of their minds through Christ.

- Lift up church leaders, asking God to give them the mind of Christ for wise leadership.

- Intercede for those who struggle with anxiety or confusion, that they may find peace and clarity in Christ.

5. Closing Prayer and Commitment

- Thank God for His transformative power that renews your mind and gives you the mind of Christ.

- Commit to cultivating a Christlike mindset in your daily life and decisions.

Daily Reflections and Insights

Today's Reflection:
How have you experienced the renewing of your mind in Christ?

Prayer Insight:
What thought patterns do you need to surrender to Christ for transformation?

Commitment Journal:
Write three ways you will actively align your thoughts with the mind of Christ today:

1.

2.

3.

Day 20: The Whole Armour of God

1. **Opening Worship**

   - Praise God for His provision of spiritual armour to protect and equip you in the battle against the enemy.

   - Sing a song like "Onward Christian Soldiers" or "Mighty to Save."

2. **Scripture Meditation**

   - Read 2 Corinthians 10:3-4 and reflect on the divine power of the weapons God has given you to demolish strongholds.

   - Read Ephesians 6:10-18 and meditate on each piece of the armour of God, asking God to help you put them on daily.

   - Read Revelation 12:12 and consider the victory we have in Christ, knowing that the devil's time is short.

3. **Personal Prayers**

   - Pray for the strength to put on the full armour of God each day.

   - Ask God to help you stand firm against the devil's schemes, wearing His truth, righteousness, peace, faith, salvation, and the Word of God.

   - Confess any areas of spiritual weakness where you have not been fully protected, and ask for God's protection.

4. **Intercession**

   - Pray for family and loved ones, asking God to protect them with His armour and give them strength in spiritual battles.

- Lift up church leaders and ministries, asking for divine protection and wisdom in spiritual warfare.

- Intercede for those who are facing intense spiritual attacks, that they may stand firm in the armour of God.

5. Closing Prayer and Commitment

- Thank God for His mighty power that equips you to stand against the enemy.

- Commit to daily putting on the armour of God and standing firm in His strength.

Daily Reflections and Insights

Today's Reflection:
Which piece of the armour of God do you feel you need to focus on more in your spiritual walk?

Prayer Insight:
What stronghold in your life do you need God's divine power to demolish?

Commitment Journal:
Write one way you will actively put on the armour of God today:

1.

"Throughout the campaign, I was praying for the healing, deliverance, and restoration of health for a close family member. During the 100 days, I saw God move, and it was evident that prayers were being answered. However, towards the final days, the situation seemed to revert to how it was before. Despite this, I refuse to accept defeat in Jesus' name. I continue to declare healing, restoration, and deliverance for my family member, and I ask for you all to join me in prayer. I firmly believe I will see a breakthrough!"

Day 21: Revealing Jesus

1. **Opening Worship**

   - Thank God for the privilege of knowing Jesus and having Him revealed to you through His Word.

   - Sing a song such as "I Want to Know You More" or "Show Me Your Glory."

2. **Scripture Meditation**

   - Read John 14:21-23 and reflect on how Jesus reveals Himself to those who love Him and keep His commandments.

   - Read John 17:24 and consider the beauty of Jesus' glory and His desire for you to be with Him.

   - Read Romans 8:29 and meditate on God's plan for you to be conformed to the image of His Son.

3. **Personal Prayers**

   - Pray for a deeper revelation of Jesus in your life.

   - Ask God to help you love Jesus more deeply and keep His Word faithfully.

   - Surrender any areas of your life that need to be conformed to the image of Christ.

4. **Intercession**

   - Pray for your loved ones, that they may experience a greater revelation of Jesus and His glory.

   - Lift up church leaders and ministries, asking for a fresh manifestation of Jesus' presence and power.

- Intercede for those who do not yet know Christ, that they may encounter Him in a life-changing way.

5. Closing Prayer and Commitment

- Thank God for the privilege of experiencing the revelation of Jesus in your heart and life.

- Commit to living in a way that reflects His glory and character in all that you do.

Daily Reflections and Insights

Today's Reflection:
How has Jesus revealed Himself to you personally in your walk with Him?

Prayer Insight:
What areas of your life do you need to surrender in order to be conformed more to the image of Christ?

Commitment Journal:
Write three ways you will invite Jesus to reveal more of Himself to you today:

1.

2.

3.

Day 22: Light & Enlightenment

1. **Opening Worship**

   - Thank God for the light of His truth that shines in your heart and reveals His glory.

   - Sing a song such as "Shine Jesus Shine" or "Open the Eyes of My Heart."

2. **Scripture Meditation**

   - Read Ephesians 1:18 and pray for your heart to be enlightened to know the hope and riches in Christ.

   - Read Hebrews 6:4 and reflect on the significance of having tasted the heavenly gift and shared in the Holy Spirit.

   - Read 2 Corinthians 4:6 and meditate on how God has shone His light into your heart, revealing the glory of God in the face of Jesus Christ.

3. **Personal Prayers**

   - Ask God to illuminate your understanding and give you deeper spiritual insight.

   - Pray for clarity in knowing God's calling and the inheritance you have in Him.

   - Surrender any areas where your heart has grown dull or blind to His light.

4. **Intercession**

   - Pray for your family, that their hearts would be opened to the light of God's truth.

- Lift up your church and leaders, that they may continue to walk in the light and share it with others.

- Intercede for those in darkness, asking God to enlighten their hearts and draw them to His truth.

5. **Closing Prayer and Commitment**

- Thank God for His light and for revealing Himself to you through His Word and Spirit.

- Commit to walking in the light, letting it guide your decisions and actions each day.

Daily Reflections and Insights

Today's Reflection:
In what areas of your life do you feel God's light shining the most?

Prayer Insight:
What specific truth from Scripture is God enlightening you with right now?

Commitment Journal:
Write three ways you will walk in the light of God's truth today:

1.

2.

3.

Day 23: Signs and Wonders

1. **Opening Worship**

- Praise God for His power to perform signs and wonders, demonstrating His greatness.

- Sing a song such as "Great Are You Lord" or "How Great is Our God."

2. Scripture Meditation

- Read Mark 16:17-18 and thank God for the power He has given to believers to perform signs and wonders in Jesus' name.

- Read Deuteronomy 10:21 and reflect on the awesome wonders God has done in your life and in history.

- Read Jeremiah 32:27 and affirm that nothing is too hard for God, acknowledging His limitless power.

3. Personal Prayers

- Pray for a fresh outpouring of the Holy Spirit in your life, empowering you to perform signs and wonders in Jesus' name.

- Ask God to increase your faith to believe in the miraculous and to move in His power.

- Surrender any doubts or limitations in your heart, trusting in God's ability to do the impossible.

4. Intercession

- Pray for your family and friends, that they may experience the power of God's signs and wonders in their lives.

- Lift up your church, asking for a mighty move of the Holy Spirit and for God to display His power in their midst.

- Intercede for those who need healing or deliverance, praying for signs and wonders to accompany the gospel and bring them to salvation.

5. **Closing Prayer and Commitment**

   - Thank God for His power and for the signs and wonders He works in your life.

   - Commit to stepping out in faith and obedience, believing that God will continue to demonstrate His power through you.

Daily Reflections and Insights

Today's Reflection:
What signs and wonders have you experienced in your own life that testify to God's power?

Prayer Insight:
What specific area of your life do you need to trust God for a miracle today?

Commitment Journal:
Write one way you will step out in faith to see signs and wonders in your life today:

1.

Day 24: The Gifts of the Holy Spirit

1. **Opening Worship**

   - Praise God for the gifts of the Holy Spirit and His divine power that equips us for godliness and service.

   - Sing a song such as "Holy Spirit You Are Welcome Here" or "Come Holy Spirit."

2. **Scripture Meditation**

   - Read 2 Peter 1:3 and thank God for providing everything we need for life and godliness through His divine power.

   - Read Romans 12:3-8 and reflect on how each believer has been given gifts according to God's grace to serve the body of Christ.

   - Read 1 Corinthians 12:4-11 and acknowledge the variety of gifts the Holy Spirit gives, and thank God for the gifts He has placed within you.

3. **Personal Prayers**

   - Ask God to reveal to you the gifts of the Holy Spirit that He has bestowed upon you.

   - Pray for wisdom to use your gifts for the building up of the church and for the common good.

   - Surrender your gifts to God, asking for His guidance on how to use them to glorify Him and bless others.

4. **Intercession**

   - Pray for your church community, asking that the Holy Spirit would stir up the gifts within each member, so they may serve with passion and purpose.

- Lift up those who are yet to discover or use their spiritual gifts, that they may be empowered to walk in their calling.

- Intercede for the global church, that the gifts of the Holy Spirit may operate powerfully, bringing transformation and revival to the nations.

5. Closing Prayer and Commitment

- Thank God for the gifts of the Holy Spirit, and for empowering believers to do His work on earth.

- Commit to using your spiritual gifts in service to God and others, asking for wisdom and strength in fulfilling your calling.

Daily Reflections and Insights

Today's Reflection:
Which gifts of the Holy Spirit have you seen in operation in your life, and how have they impacted you?

Prayer Insight:
How can you better use the gifts God has given you to serve others today?

Commitment Journal:
Write three ways you will use your spiritual gifts to bless others today:

Day 25: The Heart of Servanthood

1. **Opening Worship**

    - Praise God for His example of servanthood, and for the privilege of serving others in His name.

    - Sing a song such as "Make Me a Servant" or "Servant's Heart."

2. **Scripture Meditation**

    - Read Matthew 23:11-12 and reflect on how true greatness in God's kingdom is defined by humility and serving others.

    - Read John 13:14-17 and thank Jesus for His ultimate example of servanthood in washing His disciples' feet. Ask for the heart to serve others with the same humility.

    - Read Ephesians 4:12 and meditate on how God equips believers for works of service, strengthening the body of Christ.

3. **Personal Prayers**

    - Ask God to give you a servant's heart, desiring to humble yourself and serve others, regardless of the task.

    - Pray for opportunities to serve those around you and for the strength to serve with joy and humility.

    - Surrender any pride or selfishness that may hinder your ability to serve others as Christ did.

4. **Intercession**

    - Pray for leaders in your church and community, asking that they would lead with a servant's heart, following Christ's example.

- Lift up those in need, both spiritually and materially, asking God to raise up servants who will minister to them.

- Intercede for the global church, that believers worldwide would walk in humility and serve others, reflecting the love of Christ.

5. **Closing Prayer and Commitment**

- Thank God for the example of Jesus' servanthood and the opportunity to serve in His name.

- Commit to a lifestyle of service, asking for guidance on how you can serve others with a humble heart today.

Daily Reflections and Insights

Today's Reflection:
How can you embody the heart of servanthood in your daily interactions and tasks?

Prayer Insight:
Is there an area of your life where pride or self-centeredness is hindering you from serving others?

Commitment Journal:
Write three ways you will serve others today with humility:

Day 26: The Name of Jesus and the Blood of Jesus

1. **Opening Worship**

   - Praise God for the power in the name and blood of Jesus, which brings salvation, healing, and victory.

   - Sing a song such as "There is Power in the Blood" or "What a Beautiful Name."

2. **Scripture Meditation**

   - Read John 16:23-24 and reflect on the authority and power given to believers to pray in Jesus' name.

   - Read Acts 3:6 and meditate on the miraculous power that comes through the name of Jesus.

   - Read Revelation 12:11 and declare the victory we have through the blood of Jesus and the power of our testimony.

3. **Personal Prayers**

   - Thank Jesus for the power of His name and His blood, which secures your salvation and victory.

   - Pray in Jesus' name over any challenges, struggles, or areas where you need breakthrough.

   - Ask God to deepen your understanding of the authority you have as a believer through Jesus' name and His blood.

4. **Intercession**

   - Pray for those who are sick, oppressed, or in bondage, declaring healing and deliverance in the name of Jesus.

   - Lift up your family, church, and community, asking for protection and covering through the blood of Jesus.

- Intercede for those who have not yet encountered the power of Jesus' name, that they may come to salvation.

5. **Closing Prayer and Commitment**

- Thank God for the gift of Jesus' name and His blood, which secures your victory.

- Commit to living boldly in faith, using the authority of Jesus' name and trusting in the power of His blood.

Daily Reflections and Insights

Today's Reflection:
How has the name of Jesus and the power of His blood impacted your life?

Prayer Insight:
In what area of your life do you need to declare the power of Jesus' name and His blood today?

Commitment Journal:
Write one way you will exercise the authority of Jesus' name and the covering of His blood today:

1.

Day 27: Conquering the Flesh

1. **Opening Worship**

   - Praise God for His power that enables us to overcome the desires of the flesh.

   - Sing a song such as "Holiness is What I Long For" or "Refiner's Fire."

2. **Scripture Meditation**

   - Read 2 Corinthians 10:3-5 and reflect on the spiritual battle against the flesh and the power of God to destroy strongholds.

   - Read 1 Corinthians 9:26-27 and meditate on the importance of self-discipline and living a life under God's control.

   - Read Romans 8:13 and declare your commitment to living by the Spirit, putting to death the deeds of the flesh.

3. **Personal Prayers**

   - Ask God for strength to resist temptations and overcome sinful desires.

   - Pray for self-discipline in your thoughts, actions, and lifestyle, surrendering your body as a living sacrifice to God.

   - Confess any struggles with the flesh and invite the Holy Spirit to renew your heart and mind.

4. **Intercession**

   - Pray for fellow believers to walk in victory over the flesh and be strengthened in their spiritual journey.

- Ask God to break strongholds in your community that keep people bound to the desires of the flesh.

- Intercede for those struggling with addictions, sinful habits, or spiritual battles, declaring freedom in Christ.

5. Closing Prayer and Commitment

- Thank God for the power of His Spirit that enables you to live in victory over the flesh.

- Commit to daily surrender and spiritual discipline, walking in the Spirit and rejecting the works of the flesh.

Daily Reflections and Insights

Today's Reflection:
What are the biggest struggles of the flesh that hinder your spiritual growth?

Prayer Insight:
How can you take practical steps to live by the Spirit and conquer the flesh daily?

Commitment Journal:
Write one area where you will exercise self-discipline and rely on the Holy Spirit today:

1.

Day 28: Dreams and Visions

1. **Opening Worship**

   - Praise God for His ability to communicate through dreams and visions.

   - Sing a worship song like "Open the Eyes of My Heart" or "Spirit Break Out."

2. **Scripture Meditation**

   - Read Acts 2:17 and reflect on God's promise to pour out His Spirit, leading to prophetic dreams and visions.

   - Read Job 33:14-18 and meditate on how God speaks through dreams to guide, warn, and protect us.

   - Read Numbers 12:6 and acknowledge that God reveals Himself to His people through dreams and visions.

3. **Personal Prayers**

   - Ask God to give you clarity and discernment regarding any dreams or visions He has given you.

   - Pray for a heart that is receptive to divine revelation and a mind that aligns with God's will.

   - Ask for wisdom to distinguish between God-given dreams and distractions from the enemy.

4. **Intercession**

   - Pray for those who seek direction from God through dreams and visions, that they may receive clear understanding.

   - Ask for spiritual discernment for leaders, pastors, and intercessors who receive prophetic insights.

- Intercede for the global church, that believers may be sensitive to God's voice in this way.

5. **Closing Prayer and Commitment**

- Thank God for speaking through dreams and visions and for His continuous guidance.

- Commit to seeking Him through prayer and scripture to understand His messages more clearly.

Daily Reflections and Insights

Today's Reflection:
Have you ever had a dream or vision that you believe was from God? How did it impact you?

Prayer Insight:
What steps can you take to become more spiritually attentive to God's messages in your life?

Commitment Journal:
Write down any dreams or visions you believe may have spiritual significance and pray for discernment:

1.

2.

3.

Day 29: The Grace of God

1. Opening Worship

- Thank God for His abundant grace that sustains and strengthens us.

- Sing a worship song like "Amazing Grace" or "Your Grace is Enough."

2. Scripture Meditation

- Read 2 Corinthians 9:8 – Reflect on how God's grace empowers us to abound in good works.

- Read 2 Timothy 1:9 – Meditate on the truth that we are saved by grace, not by our works.

- Read Isaiah 40:31 – Consider how grace renews our strength when we place our hope in the Lord.

3. Personal Prayers

- Thank God for His grace that saves, sustains, and strengthens you daily.

- Ask God to help you rely on His grace rather than your own strength.

- Confess any areas where you have struggled to accept or extend grace to others.

4. Intercession

- Pray for those who feel burdened by legalism, that they may experience the freedom of grace.

- Ask for God's grace to be evident in your family, church, and community.

- Intercede for new believers, that they may grow in the understanding of God's grace.

5. Closing Prayer and Commitment

- Thank God for His unmerited favour and the power of grace in your life.

- Commit to living a life that reflects God's grace in your words and actions.

Daily Reflections and Insights

Today's Reflection:
How has God's grace shaped your life and faith journey?

Prayer Insight:
In what areas do you need to trust more in God's grace rather than your own efforts?

Commitment Journal:
Write down moments where you have clearly seen God's grace at work in your life:

1.

2.

3.

Day 30: Embracing God's Peace and Rest

1. **Opening Worship**

    - Thank God for being the source of true peace and rest.

    - Sing or meditate on a song like "It Is Well with My Soul" or "Peace Be Still."

2. **Scripture Meditation**

    - Read Psalm 4:8 – Reflect on how God provides safety and peace as we rest.

    - Read Psalm 127:2 – Consider how God's provision allows us to rest without worry.

    - Read Isaiah 26:3 – Meditate on how trusting in God keeps us in perfect peace.

3. **Personal Prayers**

    - Thank God for His peace that surpasses all understanding.

    - Confess any anxieties or burdens that are keeping you from experiencing His rest.

    - Ask the Holy Spirit to help you trust in God's promises and not be consumed by stress.

4. **Intercession**

    - Pray for those struggling with anxiety, restlessness, or sleeplessness.

    - Ask God to bring peace to families, communities, and nations in turmoil.

- Intercede for those who are weary from work or ministry, that they may find true rest in Christ.

5. Closing Prayer and Commitment

- Declare God's peace over your heart and mind.

- Commit to surrendering your worries to Him daily and embracing His rest.

Daily Reflections and Insights

Today's Reflection:
What areas of your life do you need to surrender to experience God's peace and rest fully?

Prayer Insight:
How can you make space in your daily routine to rest in God's presence?

Commitment Journal:
Write down ways you will intentionally embrace God's peace this week:

1.

2.

3.

"Before the 100 Days of Prayer, I struggled with unforgiveness, complacency, and procrastination. However, through this journey, I have learned to commit to reading the Word of God with intentionality. My heart now longs for a deeper, personal relationship with God, and I feel motivated to pursue Him wholeheartedly."

Lessons in Prayer

Prayerlessness is Pride

Neglecting prayer is an act of pride.

When we stop praying, we are telling God that we no longer rely on Him. We are saying we can handle life on our own.

Ephesians 6:18 urges us to pray on all occasions with all kinds of prayers. A prayerful life acknowledges that without God's help, we are incapable.

Prayer builds a life centred on God. Continually speaking His promises gives us confidence to declare His truth and see change.

Humble yourself before God. Make prayer your daily posture.

Day 31: Experiencing the Joy of the Lord

1. **Opening Worship**

   - Praise God for being the source of true and lasting joy.

   - Sing or meditate on a song like "The Joy of the Lord Is My Strength" or "I've Got the Joy, Joy, Joy".

2. **Scripture Meditation**

   - James 1:2-3 – Reflect on how trials produce perseverance and joy.

   - 1 Peter 1:8-9 – Meditate on the joy that comes from faith in Christ.

   - Romans 15:13 – Consider how trusting in God fills us with joy and peace.

3. **Personal Prayers**

   - Thank God for His joy, even in difficult circumstances.

   - Confess anything that has been stealing your joy, surrendering it to Christ.

   - Ask the Holy Spirit to renew your heart with a joy that is not based on circumstances but on God's promises.

4. **Intercession**

   - Pray for those who are struggling with sorrow, discouragement, or despair.

   - Ask God to fill your family, friends, and church community with His joy.

   - Intercede for those facing trials, that they may experience perseverance and joy through their faith.

5. Closing Prayer and Commitment

- Declare that your joy comes from the Lord, not from temporary situations.

- Commit to walking in God's joy daily, regardless of challenges.

Daily Reflections and Insights

Today's Reflection:
How can you maintain joy even in trials and difficulties?

Prayer Insight:
In what ways has God given you joy despite hardships?

Commitment Journal:
Write down three ways you will cultivate joy in your life this week:

1.

2.

3.

Day 32: Wisdom and Understanding

1. **Opening Worship**

   - Praise God as the source of all wisdom and understanding.

   - Sing or meditate on a song like "Be Thou My Vision" or "Open the Eyes of My Heart".

2. **Scripture Meditation**

   - Proverbs 4:7 – Reflect on the importance of seeking wisdom and understanding.

   - James 3:13 – Consider how wisdom is demonstrated through humility and good deeds.

   - James 3:17 – Meditate on the characteristics of godly wisdom.

3. **Personal Prayers**

   - Ask God for wisdom in your daily decisions and challenges.

   - Confess any reliance on your own understanding instead of seeking God's guidance.

   - Pray for a heart that is teachable and receptive to divine wisdom.

4. **Intercession**

   - Pray for leaders, pastors, and mentors to walk in godly wisdom.

   - Intercede for young people to seek wisdom over foolishness and distractions.

- Ask God to fill your family and community with discernment and understanding.

5. **Closing Prayer and Commitment**

- Declare that you will seek wisdom above all else.

- Commit to applying godly wisdom in your thoughts, words, and actions.

Daily Reflections and Insights

Today's Reflection:
How can you grow in wisdom and understanding in your daily life?

Prayer Insight:
What decisions are you facing that require God's wisdom?

Commitment Journal:
Write down three practical ways you will pursue wisdom this week:

1.

2.

3.

Day 33: Reflecting God's Love

1. **Opening Worship**

   - Praise God for His unfailing and unconditional love.

   - Sing or meditate on a song like "How Deep the Father's Love for Us" or "Reckless Love".

2. **Scripture Meditation**

   - 1 Corinthians 13:4-7 – Reflect on the characteristics of love and how they should manifest in your life.

   - 1 John 4:7-8 – Consider how knowing God means living in His love.

   - 1 Peter 4:8 – Meditate on the power of love to cover sins and restore relationships.

3. **Personal Prayers**

   - Ask God to fill your heart with His love, helping you to love others as He loves you.

   - Confess areas where you have struggled to love others selflessly.

   - Pray for a deeper understanding of God's love and the grace to reflect it daily.

4. **Intercession**

   - Pray for those who struggle to experience love due to past hurts or rejection.

   - Ask God to strengthen marriages, families, and friendships with His love.

- Intercede for your church and community to be a reflection of Christ's love.

5. Closing Prayer and Commitment

- Declare your desire to walk in love, even in challenging situations.

- Commit to being patient, kind, and forgiving in your relationships.

Daily Reflections and Insights

Today's Reflection:
In what areas of your life do you need to grow in reflecting God's love?

Prayer Insight:
Who in your life needs to experience God's love through you today?

Commitment Journal:
Write down three practical ways you will show God's love this week:

1.

2.

3.

Day 34: Contending for Light

1. **Opening Worship**

    - Thank God for being the Light that shines in darkness.

    - Sing or meditate on a song like *"Light of the World"* or *"Way Maker"*.

2. **Scripture Meditation**

    - **Matthew 4:16** – Acknowledge how Christ brings light to those in darkness.

    - John 9:5 – Reflect on Jesus as the Light of the world.

    - Micah 7:8 – Declare that God is your light even in dark times.

3. **Personal Prayers**

    - Ask God to expose any areas of darkness in your life and fill them with His light.

    - Pray for strength to stand firm in the truth despite challenges.

    - Seek God's guidance in being a light to others around you.

4. **Intercession**

    - Pray for those trapped in spiritual darkness to encounter the light of Christ.

    - Ask God to shine His light in your community, bringing transformation and revival.

    - Intercede for those struggling with doubt, fear, or despair, that they may see the light of hope.

5. **Closing Prayer and Commitment**

- Declare that you will walk in the light of Christ daily.

- Commit to standing against darkness by living in truth and righteousness.

Daily Reflections and Insights

Today's Reflection:
Where in your life do you need God's light to shine?

Prayer Insight:
How can you be a light to someone this week?

Commitment Journal:
Write down three ways you will reflect God's light in your daily life:

1.

2.

3.

Day 35: A Transformed Vessel

1. **Opening Worship**

   - Thank God for His transforming power in your life.

   - Sing or meditate on a song like *"Refiner's Fire"* or *"Make Me a Vessel"*.

2. **Scripture Meditation**

   - 2 Corinthians 5:17 – Acknowledge that you are a new creation in Christ.

   - Galatians 2:20 – Reflect on living by faith with Christ dwelling in you.

   - 2 Corinthians 3:18 – Pray for continuous transformation into Christ's image.

3. **Personal Prayers**

   - Surrender every area of your life to God for transformation.

   - Ask the Holy Spirit to help you walk in your new identity in Christ.

   - Pray for a renewed mind and heart, leaving behind old habits and sins.

4. **Intercession**

   - Pray for believers struggling with their faith, that they may embrace transformation.

   - Ask God to transform your family, church, and community to reflect Christ.

   - Intercede for those who feel stuck in past failures, that they may step into the new life in Christ.

5. Closing Prayer and Commitment

- Declare that you are a transformed vessel, ready for God's use.

- Commit to walking daily in faith, allowing God to mould you into His image.

Daily Reflections and Insights

Today's Reflection:
What areas of your life need transformation by the Holy Spirit?

Prayer Insight:
How can you partner with God in the process of becoming more like Christ?

Commitment Journal:
Write down one step you will take to live as a transformed vessel:

1.

Day 36: Divine Dominion

1. **Opening Worship**

   - Thank God for the dominion and authority He has given to His children.

   - Declare His sovereignty over your life, family, and circumstances.

2. **Scripture Meditation**

   - Psalms 8:4-6 – Reflect on God's divine plan for man to have dominion over creation.

   - Ephesians 1:18-21 – Pray for spiritual enlightenment to walk in the power and authority given through Christ.

   - Romans 6:13-14 – Surrender your life as an instrument of righteousness, rejecting the dominion of sin.

3. **Personal Prayers**

   - Ask God to help you walk in the dominion He has given you through Christ.

   - Renounce every fear, insecurity, or stronghold that hinders your authority in Christ.

   - Pray for the discipline to submit yourself to God's will, resisting sin and temptation.

4. **Intercession**

   - Pray for the church to rise in its authority and influence in the world.

   - Intercede for those struggling with spiritual oppression, that they may experience victory.

- Pray for your family and community to walk in God's divine dominion over sin, fear, and darkness.

5. **Closing Prayer and Commitment**

   - Declare that you are seated with Christ in heavenly places, above all powers and dominion.

   - Commit to living in righteousness, exercising the authority given to you by God.

Daily Reflections and Insights

Today's Reflection:
How can you exercise the dominion God has given you in your daily life?

Prayer Insight:
What areas in your life need to be surrendered to God's authority?

Commitment Journal:
Write down one way you will walk in divine dominion today:

1.

Day 37: Revealing Jesus in Me

1. **Opening Worship**

   - Praise God for the privilege of knowing Christ and being transformed into His likeness.

   - Thank the Holy Spirit for guiding you into all truth and revealing Jesus to you.

2. **Scripture Meditation**

   - John 16:13-14 – Pray for the Holy Spirit to reveal more of Christ in your life.

   - Luke 24:30-32 – Ask for spiritual insight to recognise Jesus in your daily walk.

   - Romans 8:18-19 – Surrender to the process of transformation, knowing that the glory of Christ is being revealed in you.

3. **Personal Prayers**

   - Ask God to make your life a reflection of Jesus in character, love, and truth.

   - Pray for the Holy Spirit's guidance to help you live in obedience and faith.

   - Seek God's help in overcoming anything that dims the revelation of Christ in you.

4. **Intercession**

   - Pray for your family, friends, and community to experience Jesus through you.

   - Intercede for the church to shine as a beacon of Christ's love and power in the world.

- Ask God to raise up more believers who will boldly reveal Jesus in their daily lives.

5. **Closing Prayer and Commitment**

- Declare your desire to live as a vessel that reveals Jesus to the world.

- Commit to walking in truth, humility, and love, allowing Christ to shine through you.

Daily Reflections and Insights

Today's Reflection:
How can you live in a way that reveals Jesus to those around you?

Prayer Insight:
What areas of your life need greater alignment with Christ so that He is revealed in you?

Commitment Journal:
Write down one way you will reveal Jesus in your daily interactions today:

1.

Day 38: Greater Spiritual Revelation

1. **Opening Worship**

   - Praise God for revealing Himself through Christ and His Word.

   - Thank the Holy Spirit for bringing wisdom and understanding.

2. **Scripture Meditation**

   - Ephesians 1:16-18 – Pray for the Spirit of wisdom and revelation to know God more deeply.

   - John 1:14, 16 – Ask God to help you experience the fullness of Christ's grace and truth.

   - Hebrews 1:2-4 – Reflect on Jesus as the radiance of God's glory and seek to grow in deeper revelation of Him.

3. **Personal Prayers**

   - Ask God to open the eyes of your heart to understand His calling and inheritance.

   - Pray for a hunger for deeper spiritual knowledge and insight.

   - Seek greater clarity in hearing God's voice and discerning His will.

4. **Intercession**

   - Pray for the church to walk in spiritual wisdom and revelation.

   - Ask for spiritual awakening and understanding in your family and community.

- Intercede for believers to grow in their knowledge of Christ and walk in His fullness.

5. **Closing Prayer and Commitment**

- Thank God for His continual revelation and commit to seeking Him daily.

- Declare your willingness to grow in wisdom and understanding of His truth.

Daily Reflections and Insights

Today's Reflection:
How has God been revealing Himself to you lately?

Prayer Insight:
What specific area of your life do you need greater spiritual revelation in?

Commitment Journal:
Write down one step you will take today to seek deeper spiritual revelation:

1.

Day 39: Favour with God and Men

1. **Opening Worship**

   - Thank God for His grace and favour in your life.

   - Worship Him for His faithfulness and for bestowing favour upon His children.

2. **Scripture Meditation**

   - Luke 2:52 – Pray for growth in wisdom, stature, and favour with both God and people.

   - Proverbs 3:3-4 – Ask God to help you walk in steadfast love and faithfulness, leading to favour and success.

   - Psalms 84:11-12 – Declare God as your sun and shield, trusting in Him for favour and honour.

3. **Personal Prayers**

   - Seek God's favour in your spiritual growth, relationships, and daily endeavours.

   - Pray for wisdom and integrity to walk in a way that attracts divine and human favour.

   - Ask for God's guidance in your decisions so that they align with His will.

4. **Intercession**

   - Pray for favour over your family, friends, and community.

   - Intercede for your workplace, church, and nation to experience divine favour.

   - Ask God to grant favour to those seeking employment, opportunities, or breakthroughs.

5. Closing Prayer and Commitment

- Thank God for His continuous favour and commit to walking in His ways.

- Declare that His favour will open doors that no man can shut.

Daily Reflections and Insights

Today's Reflection:
In what areas of your life do you need God's favour?

Prayer Insight:
How can you walk in greater faithfulness and love to attract divine and human favour?

Commitment Journal:
Write down one practical way you will demonstrate love, faithfulness, and integrity today:

1.

Day 40: Prophetic Declarations

1. **Opening Worship**

   - Praise God for the power and authority of His Word.

   - Thank Him for giving us the ability to declare His promises over our lives.

2. **Scripture Meditation**

   - Hebrews 4:12 – Acknowledge the power of God's Word to transform and discern the heart.

   - 2 Peter 1:18-20 – Declare that the prophetic word is a guiding light in your life.

   - Isaiah 55:11 – Proclaim that God's Word will accomplish what He pleases and will not return void.

3. **Personal Prophetic Declarations**

   - Declare victory over sin, fear, and doubt in your life.

   - Speak blessings over your family, work, ministry, and future.

   - Prophesy divine favour, health, wisdom, and breakthrough according to God's promises.

4. **Intercession**

   - Declare God's Word over your church and community.

   - Pray for prophetic insight and discernment for leaders and believers.

   - Speak forth revival and transformation in your nation through God's truth.

5. Closing Prayer and Commitment

- Thank God for the authority He has given you through His Word.

- Commit to daily speaking and declaring His promises over every area of your life.

Daily Reflections and Insights

Today's Reflection:
What specific prophetic promises from Scripture do you need to declare over your life today?

Prayer Insight:
How can you increase your faith in the power of God's Word through daily declarations?

Commitment Journal:
Write down three prophetic declarations you will speak over your life today:

1.

2.

3.

"My life has experienced tremendous spiritual growth and nurturing during the 100 Days of Prayer. Discovering my gifts has been an eye-opener, allowing me to see how much God has protected me. Being prayerful has continually granted me favour, acceptance, forgiveness, and wisdom. I am deeply grateful and will forever remain faithful to Him."

Day 41: Our Bond with God

1. **Opening Worship**

   - Praise God for His unwavering love and commitment to us.

   - Thank Him for being our Redeemer and the One who calls us His own.

2. **Scripture Meditation**

   - Isaiah 54:2-3 – Pray for spiritual enlargement, growth, and fruitfulness in your life.

   - Isaiah 54:4 – Declare freedom from past shame and embrace God's restoration.

   - Isaiah 54:5-6 – Meditate on God as our divine covenant partner who will never forsake us.

3. **Strengthening Your Relationship with God**

   - Ask God to deepen your intimacy with Him.

   - Surrender any fears, doubts, or insecurities that hinder your bond with Him.

   - Seek His presence and guidance in every aspect of your life.

4. **Intercession**

   - Pray for believers to grow in their relationship with God and experience His faithfulness.

   - Intercede for those who feel abandoned or distant from God, that they may encounter His love.

- Declare restoration over families, churches, and communities in their spiritual walk.

5. **Closing Prayer and Commitment**

- Thank God for the unbreakable bond you have with Him.

- Commit to trusting His promises and walking in faith, free from fear and shame.

Daily Reflections and Insights

Today's Reflection:
How can you deepen your personal relationship with God and trust Him more fully?

Prayer Insight:
What areas of your life need to be fully surrendered to God for a stronger bond with Him?

Commitment Journal:
Write down one step you will take today to strengthen your connection with God:

1.

Day 42: Drawing Near to God

1. **Opening Worship**

   - Praise God for His invitation to draw near to Him.

   - Thank Him for the free gift of grace and the abundance of His presence.

2. **Scripture Meditation**

   - Isaiah 55:1-2 – Pray for a deeper thirst for God's presence and true spiritual nourishment.

   - Isaiah 55:3-4 – Ask God to renew His covenant in your life and guide you as His witness.

   - Isaiah 55:5-6 – Seek God wholeheartedly, calling on Him while He is near.

3. **Seeking God in Daily Life**

   - Pray for the discipline to spend time in His Word and in prayer.

   - Ask God to reveal distractions or barriers that hinder your relationship with Him.

   - Surrender areas where you have sought fulfilment outside of God.

4. **Intercession**

   - Pray for others to experience a deeper hunger for God's presence.

   - Intercede for those who feel distant from God, that they may return to Him.

- Declare spiritual revival in your family, church, and community.

5. **Closing Prayer and Commitment**

- Thank God for drawing you closer to Him.

- Commit to seeking Him daily and prioritising His presence in your life.

Daily Reflections and Insights

Today's Reflection:
What steps can you take to intentionally draw near to God today?

Prayer Insight:
Are there things in your life that you have prioritised over God's presence?

Commitment Journal:
Write down one practical way you will seek God more deeply today:

1.

Day 43: Repairing the Temple

1. **Opening Worship**

    - Praise God for His healing power and His ability to restore what has been broken.

    - Thank Him for sending His Spirit to heal the broken-hearted and bring liberty to the captives.

2. **Scripture Meditation**

    - Isaiah 61:1 – Reflect on how God has anointed you for His work and mission. Pray for His Spirit to move powerfully in your life.

    - Isaiah 61:2-3 – Declare beauty for ashes and joy for mourning. Ask God to turn areas of sorrow in your life into places of restoration.

    - Isaiah 61:4-5 – Pray for the rebuilding of the ruins in your life, family, and community. Ask God to use you as part of the restoration process in the lives of others.

3. **Personal Restoration**

    - Pray for God's healing in your own heart, mind, and soul.

    - Surrender any brokenness or past hurts to God for His restoration.

    - Ask God to repair areas where your spiritual temple has been damaged and needs His touch.

4. **Intercession for Others**

    - Pray for those around you who are in need of healing, restoration, and freedom in Christ.

- Ask God to comfort those who are mourning and replace their heaviness with His peace.

- Intercede for the rebuilding of your community, the church, and your nation—may the Lord raise up those who will repair the desolations of many generations.

5. **Closing Prayer and Commitment**

- Thank God for His restoring work in your life and commit to being a vessel of healing and restoration for others.

- Commit to actively participating in the rebuilding of broken lives and communities.

Daily Reflections and Insights

Today's Reflection:
What are some areas in your life or community that need God's restoration and repair?

Prayer Insight:
How can you be a part of the healing process for others today?

Commitment Journal:
Write down a specific area in your life or the lives of others that you will ask God to repair and restore today:

1.

Day 44: Blessings for Obedience

1. **Opening Worship**

   - Praise God for His faithfulness and the promise of blessings that follow obedience to His Word.

   - Thank Him for the opportunity to live in alignment with His will and experience His abundant blessings.

2. **Scripture Meditation**

   - Deuteronomy 28:1-2 – Reflect on the power of obedience to God's voice and commandments. Ask God to help you walk in His will and receive the blessings He has promised.

   - Deuteronomy 28:3-4 – Pray for God's blessings in every area of your life: in your work, family, and personal endeavours. Ask for His favour to rest upon you and your loved ones.

   - Deuteronomy 28:5-6 – Declare God's blessings in your comings and goings, your home, and your future. Ask for His provision and protection to overflow in every aspect of your life.

3. **Personal Commitment to Obedience**

   - Ask the Holy Spirit to reveal areas of your life where obedience is lacking and to empower you to follow God's commands wholeheartedly.

   - Surrender any areas of disobedience or resistance to God and ask for His strength to walk in His ways.

4. **Intercession for Others**

- Pray for your family, friends, and community to walk in obedience to God's Word and receive the blessings of obedience.

- Lift up your church and nation, asking for a spirit of obedience to God to transform lives and bring forth His blessings.

5. **Closing Prayer and Thanksgiving**

- Thank God for His promises and the blessings that come from obeying His voice.

- Commit to living in obedience and trusting God to bring forth His abundant blessings in your life.

Daily Reflections and Insights

Today's Reflection:
How have you seen God's blessings manifest in your life when you have walked in obedience to Him?

Prayer Insight:
What specific area of obedience is God calling you to grow in today?

Commitment Journal:
Write down one specific step you will take today to obey God and walk in His blessings:

1.

Day 45: Revival

1. **Opening Worship**

   - Begin with worship, adoring God for His power to revive and restore.

   - Thank Him for His ability to breathe life into dry bones and restore hope and strength to the weary.

2. **Scripture Meditation**

   - Psalm 73:25-26, 28 – Reflect on the desire to be near God, finding your strength and refuge in Him. Pray that God will renew your passion for His presence and give you strength in times of weakness.

   - Ezekiel 37:4-6 – Prophesy over your own life and circumstances. Ask God to breathe His breath into dry areas of your heart, dreams, and relationships, and to bring revival where there is deadness.

   - Psalm 80:17-19 – Pray for personal and corporate revival. Ask God to restore His people, strengthen those in need, and bring forth a revival that will bring glory to His name.

3. **Personal Revival**

   - Invite the Holy Spirit to revive your heart, refreshing your passion for God's Word, prayer, and His purposes.

   - Confess any areas where you have become complacent or spiritually dry, and ask God to ignite a fresh fire within you.

4. **Intercession for Others**

   - Pray for those around you—family, friends, church members—to experience personal revival.

- Pray for a revival to sweep through your community, church, and even your nation, calling people to return to the Lord.

5. Closing Prayer and Thanksgiving

- Thank God for the revival that He is bringing to your life and for the breath of life He gives to His people.

- Commit to living in the fullness of the revival He has begun in you, trusting that He will continue His work until completion.

Daily Reflections and Insights

Today's Reflection:
In what areas of your life do you feel God is calling you to experience revival?

Prayer Insight:
How can you position yourself to receive God's revival, drawing nearer to Him each day?

Commitment Journal:
Write down one thing you will do today to foster revival in your life and heart:

1.

Day 46: Divine Protection in God

1. **Opening Worship**

   - Begin by worshipping the Lord for His faithfulness and His promise of divine protection.

   - Acknowledge Him as your refuge and fortress, the one who covers you with His wings and shields you from danger.

2. **Scripture Meditation**

   - Psalm 91:1-3 – Reflect on the safety and security found in God's presence. Declare that you trust in Him as your refuge and fortress, and ask Him to deliver you from any threats or dangers you may face.

   - Psalm 91:4-6 – Praise God for His protection and covering. Pray for His peace to guard your heart and mind, removing any fear of terror, attacks, or destruction.

   - Psalm 91:7-8 – Thank God for His promise that even in the face of great danger, His protection will not fail. Declare that no harm will come near you or your loved ones, trusting in His faithfulness.

3. **Personal Protection**

   - Ask God to surround you and your family with His protection throughout the day.

   - Pray for His divine covering over your home, work, and all areas of your life, trusting that He is your shield.

4. **Intercession for Others**

   - Intercede for those facing physical, emotional, or spiritual danger. Pray for God's protection to cover them and that they would experience His refuge and peace.

- Lift up your community, city, and nation, asking for God's protection over the vulnerable and those in harm's way.

5. **Closing Prayer and Thanksgiving**

- Thank God for His unwavering protection and faithfulness.

- Commit to trusting Him fully, knowing that under His wings, you are safe and secure.

Daily Reflections and Insights

Today's Reflection:
What areas of your life do you need to trust God more fully for His protection?

Prayer Insight:
How can you remind yourself throughout the day that God is your refuge and fortress, and that you are under His protection?

Commitment Journal:
Write down one specific way you will walk in confidence today, knowing you are divinely protected by God:

1.

Day 47: Deeper Communion with God

1. **Opening Worship**

   - Begin by thanking God for His intimate knowledge of you and His constant presence in your life.

2. **Scripture Meditation**

   - Psalm 139:1-3 – Reflect on the fact that God knows you intimately—every action, thought, and path. Praise Him for this deep connection and invite Him to reveal more of His presence in your daily life.

   - Psalm 139:4-6 – Meditate on God's complete knowledge of you. Thank Him for the peace that comes from knowing He understands you better than anyone else and is always guiding and protecting you.

   - Psalm 139:7-10 – Reflect on the inescapable presence of God. No matter where you go, He is always with you. Praise Him for His constant, faithful presence that never leaves you, and invite Him to lead and guide you today.

3. **Desire for Deeper Communion**

   - Ask God to draw you closer to Him today. Pray for a deeper understanding of His presence in your life.

   - Surrender any areas where you may have distanced yourself from Him and ask for His forgiveness and renewed closeness.

4. **Intercession for Others**

   - Pray for others to experience the deep, intimate communion with God that you are seeking. Intercede for those who feel distant or disconnected from God, asking Him to reveal Himself in powerful ways to them.

- Pray for your community and church to grow in deeper relationship with God, seeking His presence above all else.

5. Closing Prayer and Thanksgiving

- Thank God for His presence and the intimacy you share with Him. Pray that your communion with Him would grow stronger each day.

- Ask God to help you walk in awareness of His presence, trusting in His guidance and leading.

Daily Reflections and Insights

Today's Reflection:
How does knowing that God is intimately familiar with every detail of your life affect your relationship with Him?

Prayer Insight:
In what areas can you invite God to draw nearer to you today, allowing for deeper communion?

Commitment Journal:
Write down one way you will intentionally seek a deeper relationship with God today:

1.

Day 48: Deeper Service for God

1. Opening Worship

- Begin by thanking God for His call to serve Him, recognising that your life is a gift from Him. Worship Him for the opportunity to bear fruit through His work in your life.

2. Scripture Meditation

- Psalm 39:1, 4-5 – Reflect on the fleeting nature of life and the importance of living in a way that honours God. Pray for the wisdom to watch your ways and speak words that reflect His truth, especially in the presence of those who may not know Him.

- John 15:4-5 – Meditate on the vital truth that abiding in Christ is the only way to bear fruit for His kingdom. Ask God to help you stay connected to Him and depend on His strength to serve Him effectively.

- Ephesians 2:10 – Reflect on the truth that God has created you for good works. Pray that He will reveal the specific ways He wants you to serve Him and others today, and ask for the strength to walk in the path He has prepared for you.

3. Commitment to Deeper Service

- Ask God to deepen your commitment to serving Him with your whole heart. Pray that you would find joy in the good works He has planned for you.

- Surrender any hesitations or obstacles that might be keeping you from fully serving Him, and ask for His guidance in your service.

4. Intercession for Others

- Pray for others who are seeking to serve God in their unique ways. Ask God to empower them with His strength and wisdom to be effective in their callings.

- Pray for your church and community, that together you might bear fruit and serve God with unity and passion.

5. **Closing Prayer and Thanksgiving**

- Thank God for the privilege of serving Him and being a part of His kingdom work.

- Ask Him to strengthen your resolve to serve Him faithfully in all that you do, keeping your heart focused on His purposes.

Daily Reflections and Insights

Today's Reflection:
How does knowing that your life is fleeting shape your desire to serve God?

Prayer Insight:
In what areas of your life can you more deeply abide in Christ to bear fruit for His kingdom?

Commitment Journal:
Write down one specific act of service you will commit to today in your walk with God:

1.

Day 49: Deeper Praise to God

1. **Opening Worship**

   • Begin by thanking God for His goodness and faithfulness. Invite His presence into your life as you prepare to offer deeper praise and adoration.

2. **Scripture Meditation**

   • Psalm 34:1-5 – Reflect on the call to bless the Lord at all times. Commit to praising Him continually and invite others to join in worshiping Him. Reflect on the times God has delivered you from fear and filled your life with radiance.

   • Psalm 34:11-14 – Meditate on the wisdom in seeking peace, turning from evil, and pursuing good. Pray for a heart that desires life and seeks to live according to God's commands.

   • Psalm 34:17-19 – Reflect on God's deliverance from troubles and His closeness to the broken-hearted. Praise God for His faithfulness in delivering the righteous from affliction and bring to mind any current struggles, trusting in God's help.

3. **Declaration of Praise**

   • Spend time proclaiming the goodness of God. Speak out loud the ways He has delivered you, brought peace into your life, and drawn you near to Himself.

4. **Intercession for Others**

   • Pray for those in your life who are experiencing fear, affliction, or brokenness. Ask God to deliver them and draw near to them as they seek His presence.

- Pray that your community would grow in a deeper love for God, praising Him in all circumstances and continually exalting His name together.

5. **Closing Prayer and Thanksgiving**

- Thank God for His unwavering presence and His deliverance in every trial. Praise Him for His closeness to the broken-hearted and His faithfulness to the righteous.

- Pray for a heart of continual praise, remembering His goodness throughout your day.

Daily Reflections and Insights

Today's Reflection:
How does recognising that God is near to the broken-hearted influence your understanding of praise?

Prayer Insight:
What areas of your life do you need to turn away from evil and seek peace?

Commitment Journal:
Write down one way you will practice deeper praise to God today, keeping His goodness at the forefront of your thoughts and actions:

1.

Day 50: Walking in His Peace

1. **Opening Worship**

   - Begin by thanking God for His gift of peace, which surpasses all understanding.

   - Praise Him for His promise to give peace to those who trust in Him, regardless of circumstances.

2. **Scripture Meditation**

   - Read John 14:27: "Peace I leave with you; my peace I give to you. Not as the world gives do I give to you. Let not your hearts be troubled, neither let them be afraid." Reflect on the peace that Christ offers, which is different from the world's peace. It's a peace that calms the storms in our hearts.

   - Read Philippians 4:6-7: "Do not be anxious about anything, but in everything by prayer and supplication with thanksgiving let your requests be made known to God. And the peace of God, which surpasses all understanding, will guard your hearts and your minds in Christ Jesus." Reflect on how peace comes through prayer and surrender to God's will.

   - Read Romans 5:1: "Therefore, since we have been justified by faith, we have peace with God through our Lord Jesus Christ." Reflect on how your peace with God was made possible through Christ's sacrifice.

3. **Personal Prayers**

   - Pray for peace in your heart. Ask God to replace any anxiety or fear with His perfect peace.

- Confess any areas of your life where you have been troubled or anxious. Ask God to help you release these worries to Him.

- Thank God for the peace that comes through knowing Him and ask for a deeper experience of this peace in your daily life.

4. Intercession

- Pray for those around you who are struggling with anxiety or fear. Ask God to bring peace into their hearts and minds.

- Pray for your family, friends, and church community, that they may experience God's peace in their lives and grow in their trust in Him.

- Pray for the world, that peace would reign in places of conflict and unrest, and that the message of Christ's peace would spread to all nations.

5. Closing Prayer and Commitment

- Commit to seeking God's peace daily through prayer and trust in His promises.

- Thank God for the peace that guards your heart and mind in Christ Jesus. Ask Him to help you walk in His peace throughout the day.

Daily Reflections and Insights

Today's Reflection:
Where are you experiencing unrest or anxiety in your life?

How can you invite God's peace into those areas?

Prayer Insight:

How does knowing that Christ has already given you His peace change your approach to difficult situations?

Commitment Journal:
Write down three specific ways you can actively walk in peace today:

1.

2.

3.

"During the 100 Days of Prayer, I was able to forgive my relatives and rekindle the love we once shared. This experience has brought a sense of peace and restoration to my heart. Now, we eagerly look forward to having a physical meeting with my relatives to strengthen our bond even further."

Lessons in Prayer

Prayer Opens Locked Doors

Prayer aligns us with God's will and unlocks His blessings.

Philippians 4:19 speaks of God's glorious riches—His limitless provision. When we pray, we tap into this abundance.

Prayer generates power. It breaks limitations, removes obstacles, and opens doors that the enemy has shut. It invites divine wisdom, favour, and supernatural breakthroughs.

Jesus instructs us to knock (Matthew 7:7). The prayers you have been offering are knocking on doors. Keep knocking. Keep trusting. God is opening the way before

Day 51: Living with Purpose

1. **Opening Worship**

   - Begin by praising God for being the Creator and the One who has a divine purpose for your life.

   - Worship Him for His plans that are good, filled with hope and a future.

2. **Scripture Meditation**

   - Read Jeremiah 29:11: "For I know the plans I have for you, declares the Lord, plans for welfare and not for evil, to give you a future and a hope." Reflect on God's sovereign plans for your life and how He is in control of your future.

   - Read Proverbs 19:21: *"Many are the plans in the mind of a man, but it is the purpose of the Lord that will stand."* Reflect on how God's purpose prevails, even when we may face setbacks or difficulties.

   - Read Ephesians 2:10: "For we are His workmanship, created in Christ Jesus for good works, which God prepared beforehand, that we should walk in them." Reflect on the good works God has prepared for you to do and how you can live intentionally in those purposes.

3. **Personal Prayers**

   - Ask God to reveal His purpose for your life more clearly and give you a heart that is open to His guidance.

   - Confess any areas where you have strayed from His purpose or have been distracted by worldly pursuits.

   - Thank God for the good works He has already prepared for you, and ask for the strength and wisdom to walk in them.

4. Intercession

- Pray for those who may feel lost or without purpose. Ask God to reveal His plan and purpose for their lives.

- Pray for your loved ones and church community, that they would discover and live out the unique purposes God has given them.

- Pray for those who are working to bring justice, peace, and hope to the world. Ask God to guide them in fulfilling His greater purpose.

5. Closing Prayer and Commitment

- Commit to seeking God's purpose daily and aligning your actions with His plans.

- Ask for the courage to step into the good works God has already prepared for you, and to walk with confidence in His leading.

Daily Reflections and Insights

Today's Reflection:
Where do you see God's purpose unfolding in your life?

How can you be more intentional about living according to His plan today?

Prayer Insight:
How does understanding that you are His workmanship change the way you view your abilities and tasks?

Commitment Journal:
Write down three specific ways you can live with purpose today:

Day 52: Trusting in God's Timing

1. **Opening Worship**

   - Begin by praising God for His perfect timing in all things. Thank Him for being a sovereign God who knows what is best for you and when it is best.

   - Worship Him for His wisdom, faithfulness, and patience in every season of life.

2. **Scripture Meditation**

   - Read Psalm 27:14: *"Wait for the Lord; be strong, and let your heart take courage; wait for the Lord!"* Reflect on the importance of waiting on God with patience and trust.

   - Read Ecclesiastes 3:1: *"For everything there is a season, and a time for every matter under heaven."* Reflect on the different seasons in life and how each has its purpose in God's timing.

   - Read Isaiah 55:8-9: "For my thoughts are not your thoughts, neither are your ways my ways, declares the Lord. For as the heavens are higher than the earth, so are my ways higher than your ways and my thoughts than your thoughts." Reflect on how God's ways and timing are far beyond our understanding, and trust that His plans are always best.

3. **Personal Prayers**

   - Ask God to help you trust His timing, especially in areas where you may feel impatient or unsure of the future.

   - Confess any frustration or anxiety you may feel about waiting, and ask God to help you surrender your plans to His greater wisdom.

- Thank God for the seasons of life, knowing that each one has purpose and meaning in His plan.

4. Intercession

- Pray for those who are struggling with waiting, that they would find peace and strength in God's timing.

- Pray for those who are waiting for healing, provision, or breakthrough, asking God to give them hope and endurance as they trust in His perfect plan.

- Pray for those in positions of leadership, that they would trust in God's timing when making decisions that affect others.

5. Closing Prayer and Commitment

- Commit to trusting in God's timing today and in the future.

- Ask for the patience to wait on the Lord, and the faith to believe that He is working all things together for your good in His perfect time.

Daily Reflections and Insights

Today's Reflection:
Where in your life do you find yourself struggling to trust in God's timing?

How can you surrender those areas to Him today?

Prayer Insight:
How can understanding that God's ways are higher than your own change your perspective on the waiting periods in your life?

Commitment Journal:
Write down the areas where you need to trust in God's timing:

Day 53: Walking in Obedience

1. **Opening Worship**

   - Begin by thanking God for His Word, which guides us and reveals His will. Praise Him for His goodness and grace in giving us clear instructions for living a righteous life.

   - Worship Him for His faithfulness to fulfil His promises as we walk in obedience to Him.

2. **Scripture Meditation**

   - Read John 14:15: *"If you love me, you will keep my commandments."* Reflect on how obedience is a natural response to God's love.

   - Read 1 Samuel 15:22: "Has the Lord as great delight in burnt offerings and sacrifices, as in obeying the voice of the Lord? Behold, to obey is better than sacrifice, and to listen than the fat of rams." Consider how obedience is more valuable to God than outward religious rituals.

   - Read James 1:22: *"But be doers of the word, and not hearers only, deceiving yourselves."* Reflect on the importance of not just hearing God's Word but also putting it into practice in your life.

3. **Personal Prayers**

   - Ask God to reveal any areas of disobedience or rebellion in your life and give you the strength to align your actions with His will.

   - Confess any areas where you've struggled to obey God, and ask for His forgiveness and the grace to walk in His ways.

   - Thank God for the Holy Spirit, who empowers you to live in obedience to His Word.

4. **Intercession**

- Pray for those who are struggling with obedience, that God would give them clarity and the courage to follow His commands.

- Pray for the church, that it would be a community of people who not only hear the Word but live it out in their daily lives.

- Pray for leaders and decision-makers in society, that they would seek God's guidance and obey His Word in their actions.

5. **Closing Prayer and Commitment**

- Commit to walking in obedience today, asking God to help you live in alignment with His will in every area of your life.

- Pray for the strength to be a doer of the Word, not just a hearer, and to reflect God's love through your actions.

Daily Reflections and Insights

Today's Reflection:
Are there any areas of disobedience in your life that God is calling you to surrender to Him today?

How can you walk in obedience more fully?

Prayer Insight:
How does the understanding that obedience is a natural response to God's love change the way you view obedience in your own life?

Commitment Journal:
Write down three commitments to obey God in the coming days:

Day 54: Embracing God's Grace

1. **Opening Worship**

   - Begin by thanking God for His amazing grace, which has saved us, transformed us, and empowered us to live for Him.

   - Worship Him for His unconditional love and for the grace He extends to us daily.

2. **Scripture Meditation**

   - Read Ephesians 2:8-9: "For by grace you have been saved through faith. And this is not your own doing; it is the gift of God, not a result of works, so that no one may boast." Reflect on the gift of salvation through grace and not by works.

   - Read 2 Corinthians 12:9: "But he said to me, 'My grace is sufficient for you, for my power is made perfect in weakness.' Therefore I will boast all the more gladly of my weaknesses, so that the power of Christ may rest upon me." Reflect on how God's grace works in our weakness to display His power.

   - Read Titus 2:11-12: "For the grace of God has appeared, bringing salvation for all people, training us to renounce ungodliness and worldly passions, and to live self-controlled, upright, and godly lives in the present age." Reflect on how grace not only saves but also teaches us to live righteous lives.

3. **Personal Prayers**

   - Thank God for the grace that has saved you and brought you into relationship with Him.

   - Confess any areas where you have taken God's grace for granted and ask for His forgiveness.

- Pray for an increased understanding of grace, so you can walk in the freedom it brings.

4. Intercession

- Pray for those who don't yet know the grace of God in their lives, that they would experience the transformative power of salvation.

- Pray for those who feel unworthy of God's grace, that they would experience His love and forgiveness.

- Pray for the Church, that it would continually live out the grace of God and extend grace to others.

5. Closing Prayer and Commitment

- Commit to living in light of God's grace, embracing it in your daily walk and sharing it with others.

- Ask for the strength to reject worldly passions and live a godly life empowered by God's grace.

Daily Reflections and Insights

Today's Reflection:
How has God's grace impacted your life, and how can you extend grace to others today?

Prayer Insight:
How does the understanding that grace is not just about salvation but also about living a godly life influence your perspective on daily decisions?

Commitment Journal:
Write down three ways you will live out God's grace today:

Day 55: Strength in Weakness

1. **Opening Worship**

   - Begin by praising God for His strength that is made perfect in our weakness.

   - Worship Him for being our source of power and for carrying us through every difficulty.

2. **Scripture Meditation**

   - Read 2 Corinthians 12:9-10: "But he said to me, 'My grace is sufficient for you, for my power is made perfect in weakness.' Therefore I will boast all the more gladly of my weaknesses, so that the power of Christ may rest upon me. For the sake of Christ, then, I am content with weaknesses, insults, hardships, persecutions, and calamities. For when I am weak, then I am strong." Reflect on how our weakness makes space for God's strength to shine.

   - Read Isaiah 40:29-31: "He gives power to the faint, and to him who has no might he increases strength. Even youths shall faint and be weary, and young men shall fall exhausted; but they who wait for the Lord shall renew their strength; they shall mount up with wings like eagles; they shall run and not be weary; they shall walk and not faint." Reflect on how God strengthens those who wait on Him.

   - Read Philippians 4:13: *"I can do all things through him who strengthens me."* Reflect on how God's strength enables us to do the impossible.

3. **Personal Prayers**

   - Thank God for being your strength when you feel weak and for lifting you up in difficult times.

- Confess any times when you have relied on your own strength instead of depending on God's power.

- Pray for the humility to rely on God's strength in every area of your life, especially in your weaknesses.

4. Intercession

- Pray for those who are struggling in weakness, whether physical, emotional, or spiritual, that they would experience God's strength and power.

- Pray for those who feel overwhelmed by life's challenges, that they would find renewal in God's presence.

- Pray for the Church, that it would be a beacon of hope for those in weakness, offering encouragement and the strength of Christ.

5. Closing Prayer and Commitment

- Commit to embracing your weaknesses and relying on God's strength in every situation you face today.

- Ask God to strengthen you where you feel faint and to empower you to serve Him with renewed energy and purpose.

Daily Reflections and Insights

Today's Reflection:
In what areas of your life do you feel weak, and how can you allow God's strength to work in those areas?

Prayer Insight:
How does the reality that God's power is made perfect in our weakness change the way you view challenges and difficulties in your life?

Commitment Journal:

Write down three ways you will trust in God's strength today:

1.

2.

3.

Day 56: Walking in God's Peace

1. **Opening Worship**

   - Begin by praising God for being the source of true peace in the midst of turmoil.

   - Worship Him for His ability to guard your heart and mind with His peace that transcends understanding.

2. **Scripture Meditation**

   - Read Philippians 4:6-7: "Do not be anxious about anything, but in everything by prayer and supplication with thanksgiving let your requests be made known to God. And the peace of God, which surpasses all understanding, will guard your hearts and your minds in Christ Jesus." Reflect on how prayer and thanksgiving open the door to God's peace.

   - Read Isaiah 26:3: "You keep him in perfect peace whose mind is stayed on you, because he trusts in you." Reflect on how trusting in God brings peace to your mind and soul.

   - Read John 14:27: "Peace I leave with you; my peace I give to you. Not as the world gives do I give to you. Let not your hearts be troubled, neither let them be afraid." Reflect on how Jesus offers peace that is different from the world's peace.

3. **Personal Prayers**

   - Thank God for His peace that surpasses all understanding and guards your heart and mind.

   - Confess any anxiety or worry that you have allowed to steal your peace, and ask God to replace it with His peace.

   - Pray for a deeper trust in God that will lead to greater peace, even in the face of challenges.

4. **Intercession**

- Pray for those who are struggling with anxiety and fear, that they would experience God's peace.

- Pray for people in situations of conflict or stress, that they would find rest in God's presence.

- Pray for the Church, that it would be a place where God's peace reigns and is shared with those who need it.

5. **Closing Prayer and Commitment**

- Commit to keeping your mind focused on God and trusting in His peace throughout the day.

- Ask God to help you recognise when you are allowing anxiety to control you, and remind you to turn to Him for peace.

Daily Reflections and Insights

Today's Reflection:
What situations or relationships tend to steal your peace, and how can you invite God's peace into those areas today?

Prayer Insight:
How does God's peace, which surpasses all understanding, guard your heart and mind?

In what ways can you hold onto this peace in challenging moments?

Commitment Journal:
Write down three ways you will walk in God's peace today:

Day 57: Living a Life of Gratitude

1. Opening Worship

- Begin by thanking God for His goodness and faithfulness in your life. Worship Him for being the source of all blessings.

- Sing or declare songs of gratitude, remembering His acts of kindness, mercy, and grace.

2. Scripture Meditation

- Read 1 Thessalonians 5:16-18: *"Rejoice always, pray without ceasing, give thanks in all circumstances; for this is the will of God in Christ Jesus for you."* Reflect on how gratitude is an expression of God's will and how it impacts your relationship with Him.

- Read Psalm 107:1: *"Oh give thanks to the Lord, for he is good, for his steadfast love endures forever!"* Reflect on the enduring love of God and the countless reasons we have to give thanks.

- Read Colossians 3:15-17: "And let the peace of Christ rule in your hearts, to which indeed you were called in one body. And be thankful. Let the word of Christ dwell in you richly, teaching and admonishing one another in all wisdom, singing psalms and hymns and spiritual songs, with thankfulness in your hearts to God." Reflect on how gratitude is linked to peace, worship, and community.

3. Personal Prayers

- Praise God for His goodness and steadfast love, and thank Him for His continuous blessings in your life.

- Confess any times when you have allowed ingratitude or complaints to overshadow your heart and ask God to renew your spirit of thankfulness.

- Pray for the grace to live a life of continual gratitude, reflecting His love and goodness in all you do.

4. Intercession

- Pray for those who are struggling to see God's goodness due to difficult circumstances, that their eyes may be opened to His love and provision.

- Pray for the body of Christ to grow in gratitude and for this to be reflected in how we live out our faith.

- Pray for those in leadership, that they may lead with thankful hearts and recognise God's hand in their lives and ministries.

5. Closing Prayer and Commitment

- Commit to cultivating a heart of gratitude, whether in times of blessing or difficulty.

- Ask God to remind you each day of something you can be thankful for, transforming your perspective through gratitude.

Daily Reflections and Insights

Today's Reflection:
What are three specific things in your life that you are grateful for right now?

How can focusing on these blessings change your outlook on life today?

Prayer Insight:
How does gratitude open the door to experiencing God's peace and love in a deeper way?

What does it mean to give thanks in all circumstances?

Commitment Journal:
Write down three ways you will live a life of gratitude today:

1.

2.

3.

Day 58: Trusting God in the Storms

1. Opening Worship

- Begin by acknowledging God's sovereignty over every situation in your life, especially the storms you may be facing. Worship Him for His power and love.

- Sing or declare songs that remind you of God's faithfulness in the midst of trials.

2. Scripture Meditation

- Read Isaiah 43:2: "When you pass through the waters, I will be with you; and through the rivers, they shall not overwhelm you; when you walk through fire you shall not be burned, and the flame shall not consume you." Reflect on how God promises His presence and protection in every difficult situation.

- Read Matthew 14:22-33: *"But immediately Jesus spoke to them, saying, 'Take heart; it is I. Do not be afraid.'"* Reflect on the fear of the disciples and how Jesus calms their hearts by revealing Himself to them.

- Read Psalm 34:17-19: "When the righteous cry for help, the Lord hears and delivers them out of all their troubles. The Lord is near to the brokenhearted and saves the crushed in spirit." Reflect on how God is near to you, especially in moments of distress.

3. Personal Prayers

- Praise God for His unwavering presence and care, even in the most challenging seasons.

- Confess any fears or anxieties that you may have about your circumstances, and ask God to help you trust Him more fully.

- Pray for the strength to remain focused on God during times of trial, and for a deeper trust in His ability to calm the storms in your life.

4. Intercession

- Pray for those who are currently going through difficult seasons, that they may experience God's peace and presence in the midst of their trials.

- Pray for those in leadership who are navigating tough decisions, that they may trust God's guidance and be empowered by His strength.

- Pray for those who do not yet know God, that they would come to know His faithfulness and trustworthiness in every circumstance.

5. Closing Prayer and Commitment

- Commit to trusting God more fully in every storm you face, whether big or small.

- Ask God to remind you of His promises when fear and doubt creep in, and to give you the courage to walk through life's trials with faith.

Daily Reflections and Insights

Today's Reflection:
What storm or challenge are you facing right now?

How can you apply today's scripture to remind yourself of God's presence and faithfulness?

Prayer Insight:
How does trusting God in the midst of trials change your perspective on your difficulties?

What is one area where you need to rely more on God's strength today?

Commitment Journal:
Write down three areas in your life where you will choose to trust God today:

1.

2.

3.

Day 59: Resting in God's Provision

1. **Opening Worship**

   - Begin by acknowledging God as your provider. Praise Him for His goodness and faithfulness in meeting your needs.

   - Sing or declare songs of trust in God's provision, remembering that He cares for you and will never leave you lacking.

2. **Scripture Meditation**

   - Read Philippians 4:19: *"And my God will supply every need of yours according to his riches in glory in Christ Jesus."* Reflect on how God promises to meet all your needs, not according to your circumstances, but according to His abundant riches.

   - Read Matthew 6:25-34: "Therefore I tell you, do not be anxious about your life, what you will eat or what you will drink, or about your body, what you will put on." Reflect on how Jesus encourages us to trust God with our daily needs and to seek first His kingdom.

   - Read Psalm 23:1: *"The Lord is my shepherd; I shall not want."* Reflect on how God is the shepherd who guides, provides for, and protects His people.

3. **Personal Prayers**

   - Praise God for His faithful provision in your life, both physically and spiritually.

   - Confess any anxieties or worries you may have about your needs, and ask God to give you peace and trust in His provision.

- Pray for the ability to focus on God's kingdom and righteousness, trusting that He will take care of all your other needs.

4. Intercession

- Pray for those who are struggling with financial insecurity or lack, asking God to provide for their needs and give them peace.

- Pray for those who are facing challenges in their careers or personal lives, that they may experience God's provision and guidance.

- Pray for the Church, that it may be a light to those in need and a source of support to those who are struggling.

5. Closing Prayer and Commitment

- Commit to resting in God's provision and trusting Him with every need.

- Ask God to increase your faith in His ability to meet your needs and to help you focus on seeking His kingdom first.

Daily Reflections and Insights

Today's Reflection:
What area of your life do you find yourself most anxious about in terms of provision?

How can you trust God more fully in this area today?

Prayer Insight:
How does resting in God's provision change the way you approach your daily needs?

What new understanding do you have about God's provision after today's meditation?

Commitment Journal:
Write down three areas where you will choose to trust God for provision today:

1.

2.

3.

Day 60: Embracing God's Timing

1. **Opening Worship**

   - Begin by declaring God's sovereignty over time. Praise Him for His perfect timing in all things and trust that He knows what is best for your life.

   - Sing or declare songs that acknowledge God's control over seasons, both joyful and difficult.

2. **Scripture Meditation**

   - Read Ecclesiastes 3:1: *"For everything there is a season, and a time for every matter under heaven."* Reflect on how every moment in life is part of God's perfect plan and timing.

   - Read Isaiah 55:8-9: "For my thoughts are not your thoughts, neither are your ways my ways, declares the Lord. For as the heavens are higher than the earth, so are my ways higher than your ways and my thoughts than your thoughts." Reflect on how God's timing may not always make sense to us, but His ways are always higher and better.

   - Read Psalm 27:14: *"Wait for the Lord; be strong, and let your heart take courage; wait for the Lord!"* Reflect on how waiting on God's timing can build strength and patience in your faith.

3. **Personal Prayers**

   - Praise God for His wisdom in knowing the perfect timing for everything in your life.

   - Confess any impatience or frustrations you may have experienced with God's timing, and ask for His help in trusting Him fully.

- Pray for the strength to wait on God's perfect timing and to trust that He is working all things for your good.

4. Intercession

- Pray for those who are struggling with impatience or anxiety about timing in their lives. Ask God to give them peace and trust in His perfect plan.

- Pray for those in the process of making important decisions, that they may know God's timing and direction.

- Pray for the Church, that it may be patient and faithful as it waits on God's timing for revival and growth.

5. Closing Prayer and Commitment

- Commit to trusting God's timing, even when you don't understand it, and waiting patiently for His direction in your life.

- Ask God to help you embrace His timing with peace and faith.

Daily Reflections and Insights

Today's Reflection:
How do you typically respond when you feel like God's timing is delayed or different from your expectations?

How can you learn to embrace His perfect timing?

Prayer Insight:
In what areas of your life do you need to surrender to God's timing?

What have you learned about God's timing from today's prayer time?

Commitment Journal:
Write down three areas where you will trust God's timing today:

1.

2.

3.

"Thank you, youth leaders, for organising such powerful prayers. I have many great testimonies, among them:

Miraculous healing of a member of my family.

Unexpected compensation from the bank for a transaction that occurred more than six years ago.

All my children are now working or studying.

Day 61: Surrendering Control to God

1. **Opening Worship**

   - Begin by acknowledging God's sovereignty and goodness. Praise Him for being in control of all things, even when life feels out of control.

   - Sing or declare songs that celebrate surrender and trust in God's will, such as "I Surrender All."

2. **Scripture Meditation**

   - Read Proverbs 3:5-6. Reflect on the importance of trusting God completely and surrendering your own desires and plans.

   - Read Romans 12:1-2. Reflect on how surrendering our lives to God is an act of worship and that it leads to transformation.

   - Read Matthew 6:33. Reflect on how surrendering our worries and desires allows God to provide for us.

3. **Personal Prayers**

   - Praise God for His wisdom in guiding our lives and for the peace that comes when we trust Him with everything.

   - Confess areas of your life where you have struggled to surrender control, and ask God to help you release them into His hands.

   - Pray for the strength to let go of your own plans and embrace God's perfect will, trusting that He knows what is best for you.

4. **Intercession**

- Pray for those who are struggling with control and the need to "make things happen" in their own strength. Ask God to help them trust Him and surrender to His will.

- Pray for those facing difficult decisions, that they may have the courage to surrender their desires to God and seek His guidance.

- Pray for the Church, that it may be a community that fully surrenders to God's will, trusting Him to lead the way.

5. Closing Prayer and Commitment

- Commit to surrendering areas of your life where you've been holding onto control.

- Ask God to help you seek His kingdom first and trust that everything else will fall into place as you live in His will.

Daily Reflections and Insights

Today's Reflection:
In what areas of your life do you find it hardest to surrender control to God?

How does trusting Him in these areas change your perspective?

Prayer Insight:
How do you feel when you truly surrender to God's will?

What have you learned today about the freedom that comes with surrender?

Commitment Journal:
Write down one area where you will actively surrender control to God today:

1.

Day 62: Trusting God's Timing

1. Opening Worship

- Begin by acknowledging that God's timing is perfect and beyond our understanding. Praise Him for His sovereignty and wisdom in orchestrating the timing of events in our lives.

- Sing or declare songs that express trust in God's timing, such as "In His Time" or "Trust in You."

2. Scripture Meditation

- Read Isaiah 55:8-9: "For my thoughts are not your thoughts, neither are your ways my ways, declares the Lord. For as the heavens are higher than the earth, so are my ways higher than your ways and my thoughts than your thoughts." Reflect on how God's timing and ways are beyond our comprehension and how this truth invites us to trust in Him.

- Read Ecclesiastes 3:1-8: *"For everything there is a season, and a time for every matter under heaven..."* Reflect on how each moment in life has been appointed by God, and that there is a time for everything according to His perfect plan.

- Read Psalm 27:14: *"Wait for the Lord; be strong, and let your heart take courage; wait for the Lord!"* Reflect on the patience and strength that come from waiting on God's perfect timing.

3. Personal Prayers

- Praise God for His perfect timing in your life, even when you don't fully understand it.

- Confess any impatience or frustration you've felt when things didn't happen according to your timeline, and ask God for peace and trust in His timing.

- Pray for the ability to wait on God, to be patient, and to trust that He is always working for your good.

4. Intercession

- Pray for those who are struggling with waiting on God's timing, that they may find peace and strength in trusting His plan.

- Pray for those who are in seasons of uncertainty, that they would be able to rest in the knowledge that God's timing is perfect and He is with them.

- Pray for the Church, that it may trust in God's perfect timing and seek His will above all else.

5. Closing Prayer and Commitment

- Commit to trusting God's timing, even in areas where you feel impatient or anxious.

- Ask God to help you wait well, knowing that His timing is always for your good and His glory.

Daily Reflections and Insights

Today's Reflection:
How have you seen God's perfect timing in your life, even when it didn't align with your own plans?

What did you learn about patience in today's prayer?

Prayer Insight:
What is your heart's response when you think about God's perfect timing in your life?

How can you cultivate more trust in Him in the areas where you are still waiting?

Commitment Journal:
Write down three areas where you will choose to trust God's timing today:

1.

2.

3.

Day 63: Resting in God's Provision

1. **Opening Worship**

   - Start with a heart of gratitude for God's faithful provision in your life. Praise Him for being your provider in both spiritual and physical needs.

   - Sing or declare songs like "Jehovah Jireh" or "Great is Thy Faithfulness," focusing on God as the ultimate provider.

2. **Scripture Meditation**

   - Read Philippians 4:19: *"And my God will supply every need of yours according to his riches in glory in Christ Jesus."* Reflect on how God promises to provide for every need you have, both seen and unseen.

   - Read Matthew 6:25-34: "Therefore I tell you, do not be anxious about your life, what you will eat or what you will drink...but seek first the kingdom of God and his righteousness, and all these things will be added to you." Reflect on how God encourages us not to worry but to trust Him for our daily needs.

   - Read Psalm 23:1-3: "The Lord is my shepherd; I shall not want. He makes me lie down in green pastures. He leads me beside still waters. He restores my soul." Reflect on how God provides for your needs and leads you into rest.

3. **Personal Prayers**

   - Praise God for His constant provision, whether it's in your finances, health, relationships, or spiritual life.

   - Confess any anxieties or fears related to provision and surrender them to God, trusting that He knows what you need before you even ask.

- Pray for a heart that is content with what God has provided and for the wisdom to steward what He has entrusted to you.

4. Intercession

- Pray for those who are struggling with anxiety about provision, that they would experience the peace of God that surpasses all understanding.

- Pray for those in need, whether financially, emotionally, or spiritually, asking God to meet their needs and provide for them in miraculous ways.

- Pray for the Church, that it may be a beacon of provision and support for those who are struggling, showing God's love through acts of service.

5. Closing Prayer and Commitment

- Commit to resting in God's provision, knowing that He will supply all your needs.

- Ask God to increase your faith in His ability to provide and to help you trust Him fully with every area of your life.

Daily Reflections and Insights

Today's Reflection:
How have you seen God's provision in your life?

In what areas of your life do you still feel anxious about provision?

Prayer Insight:
What does it mean to "rest" in God's provision?

How can you practice trusting Him more fully in your day-to-day life?

Commitment Journal:
Write down three areas where you will choose to trust in God's provision today:

1.

2.

3.

Day 64: Walking in the Spirit

1. **Opening Worship**

   - Begin with worship, inviting the Holy Spirit to fill your heart and mind.

   - Sing or declare songs like "Holy Spirit, You Are Welcome Here" or "Spirit of the Living God" as you prepare your heart to connect with the Spirit's work in your life.

2. **Scripture Meditation**

   - Read Galatians 5:16-25: "But I say, walk by the Spirit, and you will not gratify the desires of the flesh...but the fruit of the Spirit is love, joy, peace, forbearance, kindness, goodness, faithfulness, gentleness, and self-control." Reflect on how walking in the Spirit produces fruit in our lives.

   - Read Romans 8:5-11: "Those who live according to the flesh have their minds set on what the flesh desires; but those who live in accordance with the Spirit have their minds set on what the Spirit desires." Reflect on the difference between living in the flesh versus living in the Spirit, and how this impacts your daily walk.

   - Read John 14:16-17: "And I will ask the Father, and he will give you another Helper, to be with you forever, even the Spirit of truth, whom the world cannot receive..." Reflect on how the Holy Spirit is our Helper, guiding us into all truth and empowering us to live for God.

3. **Personal Prayers**

   - Praise God for the gift of the Holy Spirit, who enables you to live according to His will and produces spiritual fruit in your life.

- Confess any areas where you have been walking in the flesh rather than in the Spirit, and ask God to help you yield to His leading.

- Pray for greater sensitivity to the Holy Spirit's voice and guidance, that you may follow His leading and walk in His strength.

4. Intercession

- Pray for others to experience the transformative power of the Holy Spirit in their lives.

- Pray for those who are struggling to live according to the Spirit, that they would be empowered to overcome the desires of the flesh and walk in victory.

- Pray for the Church, that it may be a community filled with the Holy Spirit, demonstrating the fruit of the Spirit in every area of life.

5. Closing Prayer and Commitment

- Commit to walking in the Spirit today, allowing the Holy Spirit to guide your decisions, actions, and interactions.

- Ask the Holy Spirit to fill you afresh and empower you to live for God in all that you do.

Daily Reflections and Insights

Today's Reflection:
How has the Holy Spirit been guiding you recently?

In what areas of your life do you need to yield more fully to the Spirit's leading?

Prayer Insight:
What does it mean to "walk in the Spirit"?

How can you better attune yourself to the Holy Spirit's presence in your daily life?

Commitment Journal:
Write down three areas where you will seek to walk in the Spirit today:

1.

2.

3.

Day 65: Living as Ambassadors of Christ

1. **Opening Worship**

   - Begin with worship, praising God for His work of reconciliation and inviting Him to make you a faithful ambassador for Christ.

   - Sing or declare songs like "Here I Am to Worship" or "Build Your Kingdom Here," as you commit to living for His glory.

2. **Scripture Meditation**

   - Read 2 Corinthians 5:18-20: "All this is from God, who reconciled us to Himself through Christ and gave us the ministry of reconciliation...We are therefore Christ's ambassadors, as though God were making His appeal through us." Reflect on what it means to be an ambassador for Christ in your daily life.

   - Read Matthew 28:18-20: *"Go therefore and make disciples of all nations...teaching them to observe all that I have commanded you."* Reflect on the Great Commission and how you are called to share the gospel and make disciples.

   - Read Acts 1:8: "But you will receive power when the Holy Spirit has come upon you, and you will be my witnesses...to the ends of the earth." Reflect on how the Holy Spirit empowers you to be a witness for Christ.

3. **Personal Prayers**

   - Praise God for the opportunity to be His ambassador, sharing His message of reconciliation and love with the world.

   - Confess any times when you have been timid or reluctant to share your faith, and ask God for boldness and courage to represent Christ well.

- Pray for the ability to live a life that reflects Christ's love, truth, and grace in every conversation and action.

4. Intercession

- Pray for people in your life who do not yet know Christ, that they would encounter the truth of the gospel and respond in faith.

- Pray for missionaries and those on the frontlines of sharing the gospel, that they would be faithful in their witness and empowered by the Holy Spirit.

- Pray for the Church, that it would live as a community of ambassadors for Christ, faithfully carrying out the Great Commission.

5. Closing Prayer and Commitment

- Commit to living as an ambassador for Christ today, sharing His love with those around you through your words and actions.

- Ask the Holy Spirit to empower you to be a bold witness for Christ in every area of your life.

Daily Reflections and Insights

Today's Reflection:
How can you be more intentional in sharing the message of Christ with others?

What obstacles or fears do you need to overcome to be a faithful ambassador for Christ?

Prayer Insight:
What does it mean to be an ambassador for Christ in your everyday life?

How can you reflect Christ's love and truth in your relationships and work?

Commitment Journal:
Write down three ways you can actively represent Christ today:

1.

2.

3.

Day 66: Living a Life of Integrity and Purpose

1. **Opening Worship**

   - Begin by worshiping God, thanking Him for the integrity and purpose He has given you through Christ.

   - Sing or declare songs like "I Will Follow" or "Living for Your Glory," committing to live a life that reflects His righteousness.

2. **Scripture Meditation**

   - Read Proverbs 10:9: "Whoever walks in integrity walks securely, but whoever takes crooked paths will be found out." Reflect on how integrity impacts your relationship with God and others.

   - Read Colossians 3:23-24: "Whatever you do, work heartily, as for the Lord and not for men, knowing that from the Lord you will receive the inheritance as your reward." Reflect on living with purpose, knowing that every action can glorify God.

   - Read Matthew 5:14-16: "You are the light of the world. A city on a hill cannot be hidden. In the same way, let your light shine before others, that they may see your good works and give glory to your Father in heaven." Reflect on how your actions can bring light to the world and point others to God.

3. **Personal Prayers**

   - Confess any areas where you have compromised your integrity or where you have not lived with purpose.

- Ask God for the strength and wisdom to live with integrity in all areas of your life—whether at work, in relationships, or in private moments.

- Pray for a heart that desires to glorify God in everything you do, seeking to be a light in your community and workplace.

4. Intercession

- Pray for those in your life who struggle with integrity or purpose, that they would encounter God's truth and find strength to live according to His will.

- Pray for leaders in the church, workplace, and government, that they would lead with integrity and honour God in their decisions.

- Pray for yourself and others to live lives that reflect God's love and truth, shining brightly in a dark world.

5. Closing Prayer and Commitment

- Commit to walking in integrity and living with purpose today, recognising that every action has eternal significance when done for God's glory.

- Ask the Holy Spirit to guide your decisions and help you reflect Christ in all you do.

Daily Reflections and Insights

Today's Reflection:
In what areas of your life do you need to embrace greater integrity?

How can you begin to make changes to reflect God's purpose for you more clearly?
Prayer Insight:

How does understanding that every action is for God's glory change your perspective on your work, relationships, and daily tasks?

Commitment Journal:
Write down three ways you can intentionally live with integrity and purpose today:

1.

2.

3.

Day 67: Overcoming Temptation and Staying Strong in Faith

1. **Opening Worship**

   • Start by thanking God for His protection over you in times of temptation. Praise Him for His faithfulness and His ability to strengthen you.

   • Sing songs like "Deliver Me" or "Worthy of It All," focusing on God's strength to help you overcome all challenges.

2. **Scripture Meditation**

   • Read 1 Corinthians 10:13: "No temptation has overtaken you except what is common to mankind. And God is faithful; he will not let you be tempted beyond what you can bear. But when you are tempted, he will also provide a way out so that you can endure it." Reflect on God's faithfulness in the face of temptation.

   • Read James 1:12: "Blessed is the one who perseveres under trial because, having stood the test, that person will receive the crown of life that the Lord has promised to those who love him." Reflect on how enduring temptation leads to spiritual growth and reward.

   • Read Matthew 26:41: "Watch and pray so that you will not fall into temptation. The spirit is willing, but the flesh is weak." Reflect on how staying spiritually alert can help you overcome temptation.

3. **Personal Prayers**

   • Confess any areas of temptation where you've struggled recently and ask for God's help to overcome them.

   • Pray for strength to resist temptation and a heart that desires to honour God above all.

- Ask God to fill you with His Holy Spirit to give you wisdom and strength in moments of trial and temptation.

4. Intercession

- Pray for loved ones or people you know who are struggling with temptation or sin. Ask God to deliver them and help them find freedom.

- Pray for leaders in the church and your community, that they would resist temptation and remain strong in faith.

- Ask God to protect you and others from future temptations and to give you the wisdom to recognise them before they take root.

5. Closing Prayer and Commitment

- Commit to staying vigilant in your walk with God, recognising that temptation will come but God has promised to help you overcome.

- Ask for the grace to remain faithful and strong in the face of any trial or temptation today.

Daily Reflections and Insights

Today's Reflection:
How have you experienced God's faithfulness in helping you overcome temptation in the past?

How can you rely on that truth today?

Prayer Insight:
In what areas of your life do you need to strengthen your resolve to resist temptation?

Commitment Journal:

Write down three areas where you will be more vigilant in resisting temptation today:

1.

2.

3.

Day 68: Walking in God's Peace Amid Life's Challenges

1. **Opening Worship**

   - Begin by worshipping God for being the source of peace. Praise Him for the comfort and calm He brings in the midst of life's storms.

   - Sing songs such as "Peace Be Still" or "It Is Well," focusing on the peace that passes all understanding.

2. **Scripture Meditation**

   - Read John 14:27: "Peace I leave with you; my peace I give you. I do not give to you as the world gives. Do not let your hearts be troubled and do not be afraid." Reflect on the unique peace that Jesus offers, which is different from the temporary peace of the world.

   - Read Philippians 4:6-7: "Do not be anxious about anything, but in every situation, by prayer and petition, with thanksgiving, present your requests to God. And the peace of God, which transcends all understanding, will guard your hearts and your minds in Christ Jesus." Reflect on how bringing your anxieties to God leads to peace.

   - Read Isaiah 26:3: *"You will keep in perfect peace those whose minds are steadfast, because they trust in you."* Reflect on how trust in God is the foundation for experiencing His perfect peace.

3. **Personal Prayers**

   - Confess any areas where anxiety or worry has taken hold of your heart. Ask for God to replace your anxiety with His peace.

- Pray for God's peace to fill your mind, especially in areas where you are struggling. Ask Him to help you keep your focus on Him.

- Pray for those who are currently experiencing turmoil or difficulty, asking God to give them peace that surpasses understanding.

4. Intercession

- Pray for your family and friends who may be dealing with anxiety or stress, that they would experience God's peace.

- Pray for church leaders and community leaders to have peace in their decision-making and wisdom in handling challenges.

- Ask God to bring His peace into the world, particularly in areas where there is unrest and conflict.

5. Closing Prayer and Commitment

- Commit to bringing your worries and concerns to God through prayer, knowing that He will provide peace in return.

- Ask God to help you trust in Him more deeply, so that His peace may be your constant companion.

Daily Reflections and Insights

Today's Reflection:
How does God's peace differ from the world's peace?

What specific situation in your life can you invite God's peace into today?

Prayer Insight:

Where do you need to let go of worry and trust more fully in God's provision and care?

Commitment Journal:
Write down three areas where you want to experience God's peace today:

1.

2.

3.

Day 69: Living with the Hope of Christ's Return

1. Opening Worship

- Begin by worshipping God for the hope we have in Jesus Christ, both in His first coming and in the promise of His return. Praise Him for His faithfulness and the eternal hope we have in Him.

- Sing songs like "Christ Be Magnified" or "Living Hope" as you focus on the hope we have in Christ's return.

2. Scripture Meditation

- Read 1 Peter 1:3-5. Reflect on the living hope we have through Jesus and the inheritance that awaits us in heaven.

- Read Titus 2:11-13. Reflect on how the hope of Christ's return motivates us to live godly lives.

- Read Revelation 22:12. Reflect on the certainty of Christ's return and the rewards for those who faithfully serve Him.

3. Personal Prayers

- Thank God for the living hope you have through Jesus Christ's resurrection. Reflect on how this hope changes the way you live.

- Pray for strength to live in light of Christ's return, allowing the hope of His coming to shape your actions and attitudes.

- Pray for a deeper understanding of God's promises regarding the future, and ask for faith to trust in His plans.

4. Intercession

- Pray for the Church to live with anticipation and hope for the return of Christ, and for that hope to impact the way we serve and share the gospel.

- Pray for those who are struggling with hopelessness or despair, that they would find comfort in the hope of Christ's return.

- Ask God to reveal to the world the hope of the gospel, drawing people to Himself in anticipation of His return.

5. Closing Prayer and Commitment

- Commit to living each day with the hope of Christ's return, allowing this hope to fuel your purpose and motivation.

- Ask God to help you live in a way that reflects the reality of Christ's return, as a witness to others.

Daily Reflections and Insights

Today's Reflection:
How does the hope of Christ's return influence the way you live?

In what areas of your life do you need to live more in anticipation of His coming?

Prayer Insight:
What does it mean to live a life of holiness and godliness while waiting for the blessed hope?

Commitment Journal:
Write down one area where you want to live with more hope today:

1.

Day 70: The Gifts of the Holy Spirit

1. **Opening Worship**

   • Begin by acknowledging the presence of the Holy Spirit in your life.

   • Thank God for the spiritual gifts He has given to the body of Christ for the strengthening of His Church.

   • Invite the Holy Spirit to teach and guide you in using your gifts effectively for His glory.

2. **Scripture Meditation**

   • 1 Corinthians 12:8-10 – Reflect on the diversity of spiritual gifts given by the Holy Spirit, including wisdom, knowledge, faith, healing, miracles, prophecy, discernment, tongues, and interpretation. Ask the Lord to reveal the gifts He has placed in your life and how you should use them.

   • Ephesians 4:7-13 – Meditate on the roles of apostles, prophets, evangelists, pastors, and teachers, which are given for the equipping and edification of the body of Christ. Pray for the unity of faith in the Church and the maturity of believers as they grow into the fullness of Christ.

   • Romans 12:3-8 – Consider how every believer has a role in the body of Christ. Pray for humility as you serve in your God-given capacity, and ask the Lord to help you operate in your spiritual gifts with diligence, joy, and faithfulness.

3. **Personal Reflection and Prayer**

   • Ask God to help you identify and develop the spiritual gifts He has given you.

- Pray for the right attitude in using your gifts—not for personal gain or recognition, but for the glory of God and the edification of others.

- Surrender yourself to the Holy Spirit, inviting Him to work through you to minister to others.

4. **Intercession for the Body of Christ**

- Pray for your church and fellow believers to recognise and operate in their spiritual gifts effectively.

- Ask God to raise up apostles, prophets, evangelists, pastors, and teachers who will equip the saints and strengthen the Church.

- Pray for unity in the body of Christ so that every member functions in their calling with humility and love.

5. **Declaration of Faith**

- Speak life over your spiritual gifts, declaring that you will walk in obedience to the Holy Spirit.

- Declare that God's gifts in you will not remain dormant but will bear fruit for His kingdom.

- Thank the Lord for empowering you to serve His Church with joy and diligence.

6. **Closing Prayer and Thanksgiving**

- Thank the Lord for the privilege of being used in His work.

- Ask for wisdom, discernment, and boldness to operate in your gifts as He leads.

- End with a time of worship, committing to use your gifts to honour God.

Daily Reflections and Insights

Today's Reflection:
What spiritual gifts do you believe God has placed in you?

How are you using them to serve others and glorify Him?

Prayer Insight:
Ask the Holy Spirit to guide you in identifying your gifts and walking in them with faith and obedience.

Commitment Journal:
Write down one way you will commit to using your spiritual gifts this week for the edification of the body of Christ:

1.

"Through the 100 Days of Prayer, I have experienced a renewal of my spirit and witnessed the faithfulness of God in many ways. I have also seen His healing and restoration in the lives of my mum and mother-in-law. To God be the glory!"

Lessons in Prayer

Prayer Requires Intentionality

Effective prayer demands focus.

The Bible calls us to pray in spirit and in truth (John 4:24). This requires a heart fully surrendered to God, free from distractions.

A heart devoted to God is like a tray that carries our prayers before Him. When we approach God with expectation, He responds.

A consistent prayer life brings God's promises from the spiritual realm into reality. Stay committed. Keep seeking Him until His presence transforms your life.

Day 71: The Fruits of the Holy Spirit

1. **Opening Worship**

   - Begin with thanksgiving, praising God for His Spirit working within you.

   - Acknowledge the presence of the Holy Spirit, asking Him to cultivate His fruits in your life.

   - Sing or meditate on a worship song that focuses on surrendering to the Holy Spirit.

2. **Scripture Meditation**

   - Galatians 5:22-23 – Reflect on each fruit of the Spirit: love, joy, peace, patience, kindness, goodness, faithfulness, gentleness, and self-control. Ask the Lord to help you grow in each of these areas.

   - Ephesians 3:16-17 – Pray for inner strength through the Holy Spirit so that Christ may dwell in your heart and you may be rooted in His love.

   - Matthew 3:8 – Meditate on the connection between repentance and bearing fruit. Ask God to cleanse your heart so that His Spirit can produce lasting fruit in your life.

3. **Personal Reflection and Prayer**

   - Examine your heart—are there areas where you lack the fruit of the Spirit? Confess any struggles before the Lord.

   - Pray for patience and endurance as the Holy Spirit works in you to cultivate His character.

   - Ask God to make you a witness of His love through your daily actions and interactions.

4. **Intercession for Others**

- Pray for the fruits of the Spirit to be evident in your family, church, and community.

- Ask God to help fellow believers demonstrate His love and kindness in a broken world.

- Intercede for those who struggle with anger, impatience, or a lack of self-control, asking God to transform their hearts.

5. Declaration of Faith

- Declare that the Holy Spirit is working in you, producing love, joy, and peace in your life.

- Speak life over your character, proclaiming that you will walk in the Spirit and bear good fruit.

- Declare that as you abide in Christ, His fruits will be evident in your daily walk.

6. Closing Prayer and Thanksgiving

- Thank God for His patience in shaping you into His likeness.

- Commit to walking in step with the Spirit, trusting that He will continue His work in you.

- End with a moment of stillness, listening for the Holy Spirit's direction.

Daily Reflections and Insights

Today's Reflection:
Which fruit of the Spirit do you need to grow in the most?

How can you actively surrender to the Holy Spirit's work in that area?

Prayer Insight:
Ask the Holy Spirit to reveal any attitudes or habits that hinder the growth of His fruit in your life.

Commitment Journal:
Write down one way you will intentionally demonstrate the fruits of the Spirit in your daily interactions:

1.

Day 72: Praying in the Spirit

1. **Opening Worship**

   - Begin with thanksgiving, acknowledging God's presence and the gift of the Holy Spirit.

   - Praise God for His power and the privilege of communion with Him through prayer.

   - Sing or meditate on a worship song that focuses on the Holy Spirit's work in your life.

2. **Scripture Meditation**

   - Matthew 3:11 – Reflect on the baptism of the Holy Spirit and fire. Ask the Lord to stir a fresh hunger in you for a deeper experience with Him.

   - Jude 1:20 – Pray for spiritual growth as you build yourself up in faith through praying in the Spirit.

   - Ephesians 6:18 – Meditate on the importance of praying in the Spirit at all times and in all circumstances.

3. **Personal Reflection and Prayer**

   - Ask the Holy Spirit to teach you how to pray with greater fervency and alignment with God's will.

   - Surrender your thoughts, emotions, and desires to the Spirit, allowing Him to lead your prayers.

   - If you have received the gift of praying in tongues, spend time praying in the Spirit, trusting God to intercede through you.

4. **Intercession for Others**

- Pray for a greater outpouring of the Holy Spirit in your church and community.

- Ask God to fill believers with boldness and passion for intercessory prayer.

- Intercede for those who feel spiritually dry, asking the Holy Spirit to ignite a fresh fire in their hearts.

5. Declaration of Faith

- Declare that you are empowered by the Holy Spirit to pray effectively.

- Speak life over your spiritual journey, affirming that you will grow deeper in communion with God.

- Proclaim that through the Spirit, your prayers will bring transformation and breakthrough.

6. Closing Prayer and Thanksgiving

- Thank God for His presence and for hearing your prayers.

- Commit to making prayer in the Spirit a regular part of your daily walk with God.

- Rest in the assurance that the Holy Spirit is interceding for you according to God's perfect will.

Daily Reflections and Insights

Today's Reflection:
How can you make praying in the Spirit a daily habit?

What distractions do you need to remove to deepen your prayer life?

Prayer Insight:
The more you yield to the Holy Spirit in prayer, the more you will experience His power and guidance in your life.

Commitment Journal:
Write down one step you will take to cultivate a stronger prayer life in the Spirit:

1.

Day 73: Praying in Tongues – Individual Edification

1. **Opening Worship**

   - Start with gratitude for the Holy Spirit's work in your life. Worship God for the privilege of communing with Him in prayer.

   - Sing a song that invites the Holy Spirit's presence (e.g., "Holy Spirit, You Are Welcome Here").

2. **Scripture Meditation**

   - 1 Corinthians 14:2, 4a, 13, 15 – Reflect on how praying in tongues allows your spirit to communicate mysteries with God and builds you up.

   - 1 Corinthians 1:5 – Acknowledge that in Christ, you are enriched with all kinds of speech and knowledge.

   - Acts 2:4 – Remember the Pentecost moment, when the Holy Spirit enabled the disciples to speak in tongues as a sign of His power.

3. **Personal Reflection and Prayer**

   - Ask the Holy Spirit to increase your desire for deeper communion with Him through prayer.

   - If you pray in tongues, spend intentional time praying in the Spirit, allowing Him to edify your spirit.

   - If you do not yet pray in tongues, ask the Lord to fill you afresh and lead you in the gifts of the Spirit.

4. **Intercession for Others**

   - Pray that believers in your community will grow in their prayer lives and be open to the Holy Spirit's leading.

- Ask God to give wisdom and discernment to those who desire to understand spiritual gifts.

- Intercede for church leaders to teach and guide people in using their spiritual gifts for the edification of the body of Christ.

5. Closing Prayer and Thanksgiving

- Thank God for His presence and for deepening your intimacy with Him through prayer.

- Commit to seeking Him daily, both in the Spirit and with understanding.

- Rest in the assurance that as you pray in tongues, your faith and spirit are being strengthened.

Daily Reflections and Insights

Today's Reflection:
How has praying in tongues or seeking deeper intimacy with God transformed your personal prayer life?

Prayer Insight:
When you pray in tongues, your spirit is edified and strengthened, even if your mind does not fully comprehend.

Commitment Journal:
Write down how you will make room for the Holy Spirit in your daily prayers:

1.

Day 74: Praying in Tongues: Church Edification and Gift of Prophecy

1. Opening Worship

- Thank God for the gifts of the Spirit that strengthen and build the church. Worship Him for His guidance in using these gifts for His glory and the edification of the body of Christ.

2. Scripture Meditation

- 1 Corinthians 14:1, 3-6 – Pray for a desire for the gifts of the Spirit, especially prophecy, and that they may be used for the strengthening, encouraging, and comfort of the church.

- 1 Corinthians 14:12, 22 – Ask God to help you excel in spiritual gifts that build up the church, particularly prophecy, and that tongues may be used in a way that is beneficial to the body of believers.

- 1 Corinthians 14:23-25, 39-40 – Pray that the church may operate in a fitting and orderly way, with tongues and prophecy used to convict and bring people closer to God.

3. Personal Prayers

- Seek God's help in growing in the gifts of the Spirit and their proper use within the church.

- Pray for boldness to speak prophetic words that edify others and bring glory to God.

- Ask God to help you discern when and how to speak in tongues and prophecy for the benefit of the church.

4. Intercession

- Intercede for leaders and members of your congregation to receive and use these gifts to build up the body.

- Pray for unbelievers who may be visiting your church, that they will encounter the truth and power of God through the gifts of the Spirit.

5. Closing Prayer and Commitment

- Thank God for the gifts He has given and commit to using them for the edification of the church.

- Declare that your life and your church will be a place where the gifts of prophecy and tongues build up and glorify God.

Daily Reflections and Insights

Today's Reflection:
How can you contribute to the edification of the church through the gifts of the Spirit?

Prayer Insight:
In what ways can you use prophecy and tongues to build up your brothers and sisters in Christ?

Commitment Journal:
Write down one way you will actively seek to use the gifts of the Spirit for the church's benefit today:

1.

Day 75: Guarding Against Complacency

1. **Opening Worship**

   - Thank God for His faithfulness and His call to remain steadfast in our walk with Him.

   - Worship Him for the strength He provides to persevere and avoid complacency.

2. **Scripture Meditation**

   - Zephaniah 1:12 – Pray for the ability to remain vigilant and not become complacent in your faith.

   - Revelation 3:16 – Ask God to protect you from becoming lukewarm, and to reignite a passionate desire for His presence and will.

   - Hebrews 12:1-3 – Pray for endurance and focus to run the race marked out for you, keeping your eyes on Jesus and throwing off all that hinders.

3. **Personal Prayers**

   - Seek God's help in identifying areas where complacency may have taken root and ask for a renewed zeal to pursue Him wholeheartedly.

   - Pray for the strength to cast off sin and distractions that hinder your spiritual growth.

   - Ask God to help you endure and remain faithful even in difficult circumstances, fixing your eyes on the joy set before you.

4. **Intercession**

   - Pray for fellow believers, that they would remain vigilant in their faith and not fall into complacency.

- Intercede for your church and community to be spiritually awake, alert, and eager to serve the Lord.

- Ask God to help those who may be growing weary in their faith to be encouraged and strengthened.

5. **Closing Prayer and Commitment**

- Thank God for His discipline and love, and commit to running the race with perseverance, focusing on Jesus.

- Declare your intention to guard your heart against complacency and to live each day with passion for Him.

Daily Reflections and Insights

Today's Reflection:
Are there areas of your life where you have become complacent in your faith?

Prayer Insight:
What steps can you take today to reignite your passion for God and guard against spiritual apathy?

Commitment Journal:
Write down one specific way you will actively guard against complacency in your spiritual walk today:

1.

Day 76: Walking in Obedience

1. Opening Worship

- Praise God for His wisdom and guidance in your life.

- Sing a song of surrender such as *"I Surrender All"* or *"Trust and Obey."*

2. Scripture Meditation

- Read Deuteronomy 5:33: "Walk in obedience to all that the Lord your God has commanded you, so that you may live and prosper and prolong your days in the land that you will possess." Reflect on the blessings that come from obedience.

- Read John 14:15: *"If you love me, keep my commands."* Meditate on how obedience is an act of love towards God.

- Read James 1:22: "Do not merely listen to the word, and so deceive yourselves. Do what it says." Ask God to help you not just hear His Word but act on it.

3. Personal Prayers

- Confess any areas where you have struggled with obedience.

- Ask God for the strength to follow His commands, even when it is difficult.

- Pray for a heart that delights in obeying Him.

4. Intercession

- Pray for fellow believers who may be struggling with obedience in their faith walk.

- Ask God to guide new believers in understanding His will and commands.

- Intercede for your church leaders, that they may lead with integrity and obedience to God's Word.

5. Closing Prayer and Commitment

- Declare your commitment to walking in obedience, trusting that God's way is best.

- Ask the Holy Spirit to guide your steps daily.

Daily Reflections and Insights

Today's Reflection:
What is one area where God is calling you to deeper obedience?

Prayer Insight:
How can you practically apply God's commands in your daily life?

Commitment Journal:
Write down three actions you will take to walk in obedience today:

1.

2.

3.

Day 77: Trusting God's Timing

1. **Opening Worship**

   - Praise God for His sovereignty over time and seasons.

   - Sing a song of trust, such as *"In His Time"* or *"Wait on the Lord."*

2. **Scripture Meditation**

   - Read Ecclesiastes 3:11: "He has made everything beautiful in its time. Also, he has put eternity into man's heart, yet so that he cannot find out what God has done from the beginning to the end." Reflect on how God's timing is always perfect.

   - Read Habakkuk 2:3: "For the revelation awaits an appointed time; it speaks of the end and will not prove false. Though it lingers, wait for it; it will certainly come and will not delay." Meditate on the importance of waiting on God's promises.

   - Read Psalm 27:14: *"Wait for the Lord; be strong and take heart and wait for the Lord."* Ask God for the patience and strength to trust in His timing.

3. **Personal Prayers**

   - Surrender any areas where you are struggling to wait on God.

   - Ask God to replace impatience with faith and trust.

   - Pray for discernment to recognise God's perfect timing in your life.

4. **Intercession**

- Pray for those who are waiting for breakthroughs— whether in healing, career, relationships, or ministry.

- Ask God to strengthen those who feel discouraged in their waiting season.

- Intercede for wisdom and patience for leaders making decisions that require God's timing.

5. Closing Prayer and Commitment

- Declare your trust in God's timing and His perfect plan for your life.

- Ask the Holy Spirit to remind you to be patient and rest in God's peace.

Daily Reflections and Insights

Today's Reflection:
What is one area in your life where you need to trust God's timing more fully?

Prayer Insight:
How does trusting in God's perfect timing bring peace to your heart?

Commitment Journal:
Write down one way you will actively trust God's timing today:

1.

Day 78: Walking in Humility

1. **Opening Worship**

   - Praise God for His greatness and His example of humility in Christ.

   - Sing a worship song such as "Humble Thyself in the Sight of the Lord" or "I Surrender All."

2. **Scripture Meditation**

   - Read Micah 6:8: "He has shown you, O mortal, what is good. And what does the Lord require of you? To act justly and to love mercy and to walk humbly with your God." Reflect on how humility is a key part of our walk with God.

   - Read Philippians 2:3-4: "Do nothing out of selfish ambition or vain conceit. Rather, in humility value others above yourselves, not looking to your own interests but each of you to the interests of the others." Ask God to give you a heart that values others above yourself.

   - Read James 4:6: "But he gives us more grace. That is why Scripture says: 'God opposes the proud but shows favour to the humble.'" Meditate on the blessings that come from humility before God.

3. **Personal Prayers**

   - Ask God to reveal any areas of pride in your heart and help you surrender them.

   - Pray for a heart that seeks to serve others selflessly.

   - Ask for God's grace to walk in humility daily, just as Jesus did.

4. **Intercession**

- Pray for leaders in the church and community to walk in humility and wisdom.

- Intercede for those struggling with pride or self-centeredness, asking God to transform their hearts.

- Pray for unity in relationships, families, and churches, where humility leads to peace and understanding.

5. Closing Prayer and Commitment

- Thank God for His grace in helping you grow in humility.

- Commit to putting others before yourself and seeking to glorify God in all you do.

Daily Reflections and Insights

Today's Reflection:
What is one way you can practice humility in your daily life?

Prayer Insight:
How does humility help you reflect Christ to those around you?

Commitment Journal:
Write down one action you will take today to walk in humility:

1.

Day 79: Strength in Weakness

1. **Opening Worship**

   • Praise God for being your strength in times of weakness.

   • Sing a worship song such as "You Are My Strength" or "Great Is Thy Faithfulness."

2. **Scripture Meditation**

   • Read 2 Corinthians 12:9-10: "But he said to me, 'My grace is sufficient for you, for my power is made perfect in weakness.' Therefore I will boast all the more gladly about my weaknesses, so that Christ's power may rest on me." Reflect on how God's strength is magnified in your weaknesses.

   • Read Isaiah 40:29-31: "He gives strength to the weary and increases the power of the weak. Even youths grow tired and weary, and young men stumble and fall; but those who hope in the Lord will renew their strength." Ask God to renew your strength today.

   • Read Psalm 73:26: "My flesh and my heart may fail, but God is the strength of my heart and my portion forever." Meditate on how God is your ultimate source of strength.

3. **Personal Prayers**

   • Surrender your areas of weakness to God, asking Him to fill you with His strength.

   • Ask God to help you trust in His sufficiency rather than relying on your own strength.

   • Pray for perseverance in difficult situations, knowing that God sustains you.

4. **Intercession**

- Pray for those feeling physically, emotionally, or spiritually weak, that they may experience God's strength.

- Intercede for friends or family members who are struggling with discouragement or exhaustion.

- Ask God to strengthen the global church, especially those facing persecution and hardship.

5. **Closing Prayer and Commitment**

- Thank God for His sustaining power in your life.

- Commit to relying on His strength daily rather than your own.

Daily Reflections and Insights

Today's Reflection:
What is an area in your life where you need God's strength today?

Prayer Insight:
How has God shown His strength in your past weaknesses?

Commitment Journal:
Write down one way you will rely on God's strength today:

1.

Day 80: Overcoming Procrastination

1. **Opening Worship**

   - Thank God for the gift of time and the opportunity to fulfil His purposes.

   - Worship Him for His guidance and strength to overcome distractions and procrastination.

2. **Scripture Meditation**

   - Ecclesiastes 9:10 – Pray for diligence and a strong work ethic to give your best in all that you do.

   - James 4:15-17 – Ask God for humility and the awareness to seek His will in your plans, acknowledging that His timing is best.

   - John 9:4 – Pray for urgency in fulfilling God's assignments, recognising that there is a time for action and a time to rest.

3. **Personal Prayers**

   - Seek God's help in identifying areas of your life where procrastination may be hindering progress.

   - Ask for the discipline to tackle tasks with enthusiasm, without delay.

   - Pray for a heart that desires to do the good that God has placed before you, rather than putting it off.

4. **Intercession**

   - Pray for those struggling with procrastination in their lives, that they may find the strength to take action.

- Intercede for your family, friends, and colleagues, that they may be motivated to pursue their goals and responsibilities with diligence.

- Ask God to provide clarity and motivation for your church and community to move forward in their mission and service to Him.

5. Closing Prayer and Commitment

- Thank God for the opportunity to work for Him and commit to overcoming procrastination in your daily tasks.

- Declare your intention to live with urgency, trusting in God's timing and seeking His strength to accomplish all He has set before you.

Daily Reflections and Insights

Today's Reflection:
In what areas of your life have you been putting things off? How can you take action today?

Prayer Insight:
How can you align your plans with God's will and act with urgency, knowing that there is a time for everything?

Commitment Journal:
Write down one task you will start or finish today, taking action to overcome procrastination:

1.

"Through the 100 Days of Prayer, I have gained self-control over anger and am no longer easily offended. This journey has taught me that the primary purpose of prayer is not simply receiving but transformation. I've come to understand that the condition of your heart is crucial to answered prayer—the state of the heart is the tray that serves our prayers to God.

During this time, the Holy Spirit has been incredibly attentive, granting me clarity through the word of knowledge and numerous dreams I've encountered. These revelations have deeply enriched my faith and understanding of God's will."

Day 81: Against Fear and Worries

1. **Opening Worship**

   - Thank God for His perfect peace that guards your heart and mind.

   - Worship Him for being a constant source of calm in the midst of life's storms.

2. **Scripture Meditation**

   - Philippians 4:6-7 – Pray for the peace of God to replace your anxieties and for the strength to trust Him with every concern.

   - John 14:27 – Ask God to fill you with His peace, that it may settle your heart and ease your fears.

   - 2 Timothy 1:7 – Pray for a renewed spirit of power, love, and self-control, rejecting fear and embracing the boldness that comes from the Holy Spirit.

3. **Personal Prayers**

   - Seek God for freedom from specific fears and worries in your life. Surrender them to Him.

   - Ask for courage to face challenges, trusting that God has already given you what you need to overcome them.

   - Pray for a peaceful heart that is rooted in God's promises, knowing that He is in control.

4. **Intercession**

   - Intercede for those who are struggling with fear and anxiety, that they may experience God's peace in profound ways.

- Pray for your family, friends, and community to know the security that comes from trusting in God.

- Ask for divine comfort and peace for those affected by crisis or uncertainty in your country or around the world.

5. **Closing Prayer and Commitment**

- Thank God for His faithfulness in answering your prayers and filling you with peace.

- Commit to resting in God's peace and resisting fear, knowing that He is always with you and will never leave you.

Daily Reflections and Insights

Today's Reflection:
What fears or worries are you holding onto today? How can you release them to God?

Prayer Insight:
How can you allow God's peace to guard your heart and mind in every situation?

Commitment Journal:
Write down one way you will choose to trust God with your fears today:

1.

Day 82: Against Stress, Guilt, and Depression

1. **Opening Worship**

   - Thank God for His readiness to listen and respond to your cries for help.

   - Worship Him for being a deliverer who lifts you from the depths of despair and sets your feet on solid ground.

2. **Scripture Meditation**

   - Psalms 40:1-3 – Pray for God's restoration to remove any burdens, stress, or negative emotions. Ask for a new song of praise and joy.

   - Psalms 34:17-18 – Pray for healing from brokenness, that God will be close to you in your times of hurt and despair.

   - Matthew 11:28 – Ask God for the rest and peace that only He can provide, and pray for the strength to trust Him with your burdens.

3. **Personal Prayers**

   - Seek God for deliverance from the stress and guilt weighing you down. Surrender your feelings to Him.

   - Pray for emotional healing, that God will heal your heart and restore your joy.

   - Ask for a renewed sense of peace, trusting that God's rest is enough to overcome your struggles.

4. **Intercession**

   - Intercede for others experiencing stress, guilt, or depression, that they may encounter God's healing and find rest in Him.

- Pray for your loved ones and community to experience God's presence and be lifted from their burdens.

- Ask God to provide comfort and peace to those who are struggling silently.

5. **Closing Prayer and Commitment**

- Thank God for His ever-present help in times of need and His ability to carry your burdens.

- Commit to trusting God's peace and embracing His rest, rejecting the weight of stress and guilt.

Daily Reflections and Insights

Today's Reflection:
What emotions or burdens are you carrying today that you need to surrender to God?

Prayer Insight:
How can you invite God's rest into your life today, trusting Him to lift the weight of stress and guilt?

Commitment Journal:
Write down one practical way you will rest in God's presence today:

1.

Day 83: Against Anger, Aggression, and Bitterness

1. **Opening Worship**

   - Worship Him for His ability to forgive and remove your transgressions as far as the east is from the west.

2. **Scripture Meditation**

   - Ephesians 4:30-31 – Pray for the strength to rid yourself of bitterness, anger, and malice, and to cultivate kindness, compassion, and forgiveness towards others.

   - Psalms 103:8-12 – Reflect on God's gracious and slow-to-anger nature, and ask for His help in mirroring that same attitude in your relationships.

   - James 1:19-20 – Ask God to help you be quick to listen, slow to speak, and slow to anger, so that your actions reflect His righteousness.

3. **Personal Prayers**

   - Seek God's help to overcome any lingering anger, aggression, or bitterness in your heart.

   - Pray for the ability to forgive others as Christ has forgiven you, and to cultivate a heart of compassion and understanding.

   - Ask God for peace to replace any traces of resentment or bitterness that may hinder your growth in Him.

4. **Intercession**

   - Intercede for those struggling with anger and bitterness in your community, that they may experience God's peace and be healed of their pain.

- Pray for relationships in your life that are impacted by conflict, asking God to bring restoration and reconciliation.

- Ask God to help those who are consumed by aggression or anger to find His love and forgiveness, and to be transformed.

5. **Closing Prayer and Commitment**

- Thank God for His forgiveness and His example of compassion and love.

- Commit to pursuing peace in your relationships and to choosing forgiveness over bitterness and anger.

Daily Reflections and Insights

Today's Reflection:
Are there any unresolved issues in your heart that you need to bring before God for healing and forgiveness?

Prayer Insight:
How can you practically choose forgiveness and compassion over anger or bitterness today?

Commitment Journal:
Write down one relationship where you will choose to show kindness and forgiveness today:

1.

Day 84: The Fear of the LORD

1. **Opening Worship**

   - Thank God for His wisdom and knowledge, and for the privilege of seeking His fear.

   - Worship Him for His holiness, reverence, and the opportunity to grow in His ways.

2. **Scripture Meditation**

   - Proverbs 1:7 – Pray for the humility to receive wisdom and instruction, and for a heart that embraces the fear of the Lord.

   - Psalm 34:11-14 – Ask God to teach you the fear of the Lord, and to help you turn away from evil, speak truth, and pursue peace.

   - 2 Corinthians 7:1 – Pray for the strength to purify yourself from anything that contaminates your body and spirit, as an act of reverence for God.

3. **Personal Prayers**

   - Seek God's help in deepening your reverence for Him and growing in wisdom through the fear of the Lord.

   - Pray for the desire to live a holy and righteous life, keeping your heart and actions pure.

   - Ask God to help you cultivate peace and righteousness in your daily interactions, reflecting His love and holiness.

4. **Intercession**

   - Intercede for your community and church, that they may grow in the fear of the Lord and live lives that honour God.

- Pray for those who are struggling with sin or disobedience, that they may come to a deeper understanding of the fear of the Lord and turn from their ways.

- Ask God to purify the hearts of those around you, leading them toward holiness and reverence for Him.

5. **Closing Prayer and Commitment**

- Thank God for His promise of wisdom and guidance for those who fear Him.

- Commit to living a life that honours God, pursuing holiness and peace in all areas of your life.

Daily Reflections and Insights

Today's Reflection:
How does the fear of the Lord shape your daily decisions and relationships?

Prayer Insight:
In what areas of your life do you need to purify yourself and grow in reverence for God?

Commitment Journal:
Write down one action you will take today to live more in reverence to God and pursue peace:

1.

Day 85: Asking, Seeking, Knocking

1. **Opening Worship**

   - Thank God for His presence, His invitation to come near, and His desire to speak to us.

   - Worship Him for His faithfulness in guiding and calling us to seek Him.

2. **Scripture Meditation**

   - Hebrews 12:22-25 – Pray for a heart that is responsive to God's call and a willingness to listen to Him, knowing the importance of His voice and the weight of His warnings.

   - Psalm 27:8 – Ask God to stir a deeper desire within you to seek His face, longing for His presence in all areas of your life.

   - Luke 18:1 – Pray for endurance in prayer, that you may always seek God's guidance and never lose heart, even when faced with challenges.

3. **Personal Prayers**

   - Seek God's help to stay focused on Him and to seek His presence above all else.

   - Pray for patience and persistence in prayer, trusting in God's timing and answers.

   - Ask God to open your heart to hear and receive His voice clearly, so you may be led in His will.

4. **Intercession**

   - Pray for those who are struggling to seek God or feel distant from Him, that they may find the courage and desire to draw near.

- Intercede for your family, friends, and community to have a heart that seeks God's face and listens attentively to His voice.

- Ask God to empower His people to be persistent in prayer and to trust Him as they ask, seek, and knock.

5. **Closing Prayer and Commitment**

- Thank God for the privilege of seeking His face and for His willingness to answer us when we call.

- Commit to being persistent in your prayers and seeking God's will in all circumstances.

Daily Reflections and Insights

Today's Reflection:
How do you respond when God calls you to seek His face? Are there areas of your life where you need to be more persistent in prayer?

Prayer Insight:
What does it mean for you to seek God's face? How can you make this a priority in your daily life?

Commitment Journal:
Write down one area where you will seek God's face more diligently today:

1.

Day 86: Miracles and Wonders

1. **Opening Worship**

   - Thank God for His mighty works and the miracles He has performed throughout history and in our lives.

   - Worship Him for being a God of wonders who is powerful and faithful in answering our prayers.

2. **Scripture Meditation**

   - Psalm 77:14 – Praise God for His ability to work wonders and for revealing His might among His people. Ask Him to show His power in your life and in the lives of those around you.

   - Mark 11:22-24 – Pray for increased faith, believing that when you ask God in prayer, according to His will, He will answer. Ask Him to help you trust in His ability to move mountains in your life.

   - 1 John 5:14-15 – Pray with confidence, knowing that God hears your prayers when you ask in alignment with His will. Ask for clarity on His will for your life and boldness in prayer.

3. **Personal Prayers**

   - Pray for the ability to believe in God's power to do miracles, both in your own life and in the lives of others.

   - Ask God to increase your faith, that you may pray with unwavering belief and trust in His perfect timing and will.

   - Seek God's will in your current struggles and ask for the miracles and wonders He desires to work through you.

4. **Intercession**

- Pray for those who are facing impossible situations, asking God to move mightily in their lives and perform miracles on their behalf.

- Intercede for your community, that God's power would be revealed through healing, deliverance, and provision.

- Ask God to strengthen the faith of those who are struggling to believe in His ability to perform wonders.

5. Closing Prayer and Commitment

- Thank God for His miraculous power and for always hearing our prayers when they are in accordance with His will.

- Commit to trusting in His ability to perform miracles, and to praying with faith and expectation.

Daily Reflections and Insights

Today's Reflection:
What miracles or wonders have you witnessed in your life or in the lives of others? How can you trust God more fully for the impossible?

Prayer Insight:
How does your faith shape your prayers for miracles and wonders? Are you asking God for things according to His will?

Commitment Journal:
Write down one area where you will trust God for a miracle today:

1.

Day 87: Spiritual Warfare

1. Opening Worship

- Thank God for His protection and for being your shield and refuge in times of spiritual warfare. Worship Him as the Lord who bestows favour, honour, and good things upon those who walk uprightly.

2. Scripture Meditation

- Psalm 84:11 – Pray for God's favour and protection, acknowledging that He is your sun and shield.

- Isaiah 54:17 – Declare that no weapon formed against you will prosper, and rebuke any accusations or judgments from the enemy. Stand firm in the heritage you have in Christ.

- 2 Corinthians 1:20 – Thank God for His promises, knowing that in Christ, every promise is fulfilled. Ask for a deeper trust in His word and for the strength to claim His promises in times of spiritual battle.

3. Personal Prayers

- Ask God to equip you with spiritual armour to stand firm against the enemy's attacks (Ephesians 6:10-18).

- Pray for the strength to resist temptation and to discern any lies or attacks from the enemy.

- Seek God's peace and assurance that He will always provide victory, regardless of the battle you face.

4. Intercession

- Intercede for those who are facing spiritual battles, asking God to protect them from the enemy and to give them the strength to overcome.

- Pray for your family, church, and community, that they may be equipped with spiritual discernment and protection.

- Ask God to give wisdom and victory to those who are battling fear, doubt, or oppression.

5. **Closing Prayer and Commitment**

- Thank God for His promise of protection and for being your refuge in times of spiritual warfare.

- Commit to standing firm in His promises and walking in the authority given to you through Christ.

Daily Reflections and Insights

Today's Reflection:
What spiritual battles are you currently facing, and how can you trust God more fully for victory?

Prayer Insight:
How does understanding God's promises strengthen your stance in spiritual warfare? Are there specific promises you need to claim today?

Commitment Journal:
Write down one area where you will trust God for victory over spiritual attacks today:

1.

Day 88: Thanksgiving and Gratitude

1. **Opening Worship**

   - Thank God for being your strength and shield, and for His unwavering help and provision.

   - Worship Him for His perfect gifts, acknowledging that every good thing comes from Him.

2. **Scripture Meditation**

   - Psalm 28:7 – Reflect on God as your strength and shield. Give thanks for the trust and help He offers, and respond with a joyful song of praise.

   - James 1:17 – Thank God for all the good gifts He has given you, both big and small. Acknowledge His consistency and unchanging nature.

   - Hebrews 13:15 – Offer a sacrifice of praise to God, with grateful lips, acknowledging His goodness and the many ways He provides for you.

3. **Personal Prayers**

   - Ask God to help you recognise His blessings in every area of your life.

   - Pray for a heart of gratitude, that you would always give thanks for both the big and small things He provides.

   - Thank God for His unchanging nature and faithfulness to you, no matter the circumstances.

4. **Intercession**

   - Pray for others, that they may also experience a spirit of gratitude and thanksgiving.

- Intercede for your family and community, that they would recognise the goodness of God in their lives and give thanks.

- Ask God to cultivate hearts of gratitude in your church and in the world, for His glory.

5. Closing Prayer and Commitment

- Thank God once more for His many blessings, and commit to living a life of continual thanksgiving.

- Declare that you will offer a sacrifice of praise to God daily, acknowledging His goodness and provision.

Daily Reflections and Insights

Today's Reflection:
What are some specific blessings in your life that you can give thanks for today?

Prayer Insight:
How does acknowledging God as the giver of all good gifts change the way you approach life's challenges and blessings?

Commitment Journal:
Write down one way you will express your gratitude to God today:

1.

Day 89: Clean Out the Rubbish - Confession and Renewal

1. **Opening Worship**

   - Thank God for His constant grace and forgiveness.

   - Worship Him for the cleansing power of His blood, which purifies and restores.

2. **Scripture Meditation**

   - 1 John 1:9 – Reflect on God's promise to forgive when we confess our sins.

   - Psalm 51:10 – Ask God to create in you a pure heart and renew a right spirit within you.

   - Isaiah 1:18 – Praise God for His willingness to cleanse us, though our sins are like scarlet.

3. **Personal Prayers**

   - Confess any unconfessed sins and ask God for forgiveness.

   - Seek God's help in letting go of any bitterness, anger, or hurt.

   - Pray for a heart that is open and free of obstacles to God's work.

4. **Intercession**

   - Pray for others to experience freedom from sin and bitterness.

   - Ask for healing and renewal for those who are struggling with guilt or unforgiveness.

- Intercede for your church and community to experience a deep cleansing and renewal.

5. **Closing Prayer and Commitment**

- Thank God for His forgiveness and cleansing power.

- Commit to living a life of purity, asking God to remove anything in your life that blocks His work.

Daily Reflections and Insights

Today's Reflection:
What areas of your life do you need to clean out and let go of today?

Prayer Insight:
How does confessing and repenting impact your relationship with God and others?

Commitment Journal:
Write down one area where you need to seek God's forgiveness or cleansing today:

1.

Day 90: Pray for Jesus' Glory to Arise

1. **Opening Worship**

   - Praise God for the majesty of Jesus and His unshakable glory.

   - Worship Christ for His presence, power, and sovereignty over all things.

2. **Scripture Meditation**

   - John 17:1 – Reflect on Jesus' prayer for His glory to be revealed.

   - Philippians 2:9-11 – Declare Jesus as the name above all names, to whom every knee will bow.

   - Revelation 4:11 – Worship God, declaring that He is worthy to receive glory, honour, and power.

3. **Personal Prayers**

   - Invite the glory of Jesus to fill every area of your life.

   - Pray for a deep awareness of His majesty in your daily walk.

   - Ask for the power of Jesus to arise in your circumstances, transforming your heart and mind.

4. **Intercession**

   - Pray for your church to experience a fresh revelation of Christ's glory.

   - Ask for God to reveal His majesty to your community and beyond.

- Intercede for a spiritual awakening in the world, where Jesus' glory will be seen and worshiped.

5. **Closing Prayer and Commitment**

- Thank God for the glory of Jesus and His presence in your life.

- Commit to living in a way that reflects His glory in all you do.

Daily Reflections and Insights

Today's Reflection:
How can you make space in your life for the glory of Jesus to arise today?

Prayer Insight:
What areas of your life need to be transformed by the glory of Christ?

Commitment Journal:
Write down one way you will invite God's glory into your day today:

1.

"During the 100 Days of Prayer, I ended a relationship that was pulling my spirit down, and with it, the feeling of guilt has gone. I can now feel God's presence in my worship and prayers, which I had felt was fading—perhaps even gone.

The frustration and brokenness I once felt after prayer have been replaced with joy, peace, and grace. Even though God is mighty and holy, I now truly understand that He desires to have a relationship with me."

Lessons in Prayer

Prayer as an Altar

An altar is a meeting place between God and man.

Matthew 6:6 instructs us to go into our room, close the door, and pray to the Father. This reveals that prayer itself is an altar.

Building a strong altar requires:
- Persistent prayer

- Studying God's word

- A lifestyle of fasting

- Obedience to kingdom principles

A true altar secures a response from God. Those who give themselves to prayer—like the men of old—experience divine encounters.

If you long to know God deeply, commit to a life of prayer. Every great move of God begins with a person willing to seek Him continually.

Day 91: Ask for Revival

1. **Opening Worship**

   - Praise God for His power to revive and restore.

   - Worship Him for His ability to breathe new life into dry bones.

2. **Scripture Meditation**

   - 2 Chronicles 7:14 – Reflect on God's promise to heal the land when His people humble themselves, pray, and seek His face.

   - Ezekiel 37:5-10 – Pray for God to breathe life into places of spiritual dryness.

   - Isaiah 57:15 – Worship God for being the one who revives the spirit of the humble.

3. **Personal Prayers**

   - Pray for personal revival in your heart and spirit.

   - Ask God to renew your passion and zeal for Him.

   - Pray for the revival of the Church, that it would be a powerful force for the Kingdom of God.

4. **Intercession**

   - Intercede for your community to experience a fresh outpouring of God's Spirit.

   - Pray for revival in your church, that it would impact lives and draw many to Christ.

   - Ask God for revival in the world, for His Kingdom to come and His will to be done on earth.

5. **Closing Prayer and Commitment**

- Thank God for His willingness to bring revival and transformation.

- Commit to seeking God for revival in every area of your life and community.

Daily Reflections and Insights

Today's Reflection:
What areas of your life or community need revival the most?

Prayer Insight:
How can you participate in God's work of revival today?

Commitment Journal:
Write down one step you will take to seek revival in your life:

1.

Day 92: Clean Out the Rubbish - Confession and Renewal
(Repeat Day 89)

1. **Opening Worship**

   - Praise God for His holiness, His mercy, and His grace that brings us into fellowship with Him.

   - Worship Him for His ability to cleanse, purify, and restore us when we turn to Him in repentance.

2. **Scripture Meditation**

   - 1 John 1:9 – Reflect on God's promise to forgive us when we confess our sins and cleanse us from all unrighteousness.

   - Psalm 51:10 – Ask God to create in you a pure heart and renew a steadfast spirit within you.

   - Isaiah 1:18 – Thank God that though our sins are like scarlet, He can make them white as snow.

3. **Personal Prayers**

   - Confess any sins that are weighing on your heart and seek God's forgiveness.

   - Pray for the strength to let go of any bitterness, unforgiveness, or any other sin that hinders your relationship with God.

   - Ask God to purify your heart and mind so that you may be vessels of His grace and peace.

4. **Intercession**

- Pray for others to experience God's forgiveness and cleansing, especially those in your family or community who may be struggling with guilt.

- Ask for God's mercy to be poured out on your church, that it may be a place of healing and renewal.

- Intercede for the world, praying for revival and for people to be freed from sin and its consequences.

5. **Closing Prayer and Commitment**

- Thank God for His unfailing forgiveness and mercy.

- Commit to living with a renewed heart, constantly seeking His cleansing and guidance in all areas of your life.

Daily Reflections and Insights

Today's Reflection:
Is there any sin or burden that you need to lay before God today?

Prayer Insight:
How does confession and renewal allow you to experience greater intimacy with God?

Commitment Journal:
Write down one area in your life where you will seek God's cleansing today:

1.

Day 93: Pray for Jesus' Glory to Arise

1. **Opening Worship**

   - Praise Jesus for His majesty and glory that is revealed in all creation.

   - Worship Him for His power to transform lives, inviting His glory to be made manifest in your life.

2. **Scripture Meditation**

   - John 17:1 – Reflect on Jesus' prayer for His glory to be revealed.

   - Philippians 2:9-11 – Declare that Jesus is exalted and every knee will bow to His name.

   - Revelation 4:11 – Worship God for His worthiness to receive glory, honour, and power.

3. **Personal Prayers**

   - Invite the glory of Jesus to be revealed in your life, in your actions, and in your relationships.

   - Pray for a greater revelation of His majesty and the strength to live in a way that reflects His glory.

   - Ask God to help you live with a mindset focused on Christ's glory in every circumstance.

4. **Intercession**

   - Pray for your church to experience a fresh revelation of Christ's glory.

   - Ask God to reveal His majesty to your community and bring many to the knowledge of His greatness.

- Intercede for those in your life who do not know Jesus, praying that they would come to see His glory and receive His salvation.

5. **Closing Prayer and Commitment**

- Thank God for revealing His glory to you and for the privilege of experiencing His presence.

- Commit to living for the glory of God in all you do, trusting that His glory will shine through your life.

Daily Reflections and Insights

Today's Reflection:
How can you make space for the glory of Christ to arise in your life today?

Prayer Insight:
What is one area where you want to see Jesus' glory revealed?

Commitment Journal:
Write down one way you will invite the glory of God into your life today:

1.

Day 94: Deeper Sanctification

1. **Opening Worship**

   - Praise God for His calling and choosing you as His beloved child, sanctified by the work of the Holy Spirit.

   - Worship Him for the ongoing process of sanctification, where He transforms you to reflect His holiness and likeness.

2. **Scripture Meditation**

   - 2 Thessalonians 2:13 – Thank God for His sanctifying work in your life, making you holy and set apart for His purposes.

   - 2 Timothy 2:21 – Pray for a cleansing of anything in your life that hinders your service to God. Ask Him to make you a vessel of honour, ready for His good work.

   - Acts 26:18 – Reflect on the freedom that comes from being turned from darkness to light, and ask God to continue to sanctify you by faith, keeping you in His light.

3. **Personal Prayers**

   - Ask God to reveal areas of your life that need deeper sanctification, where you still need to grow in His holiness.

   - Pray for a continual desire to be cleansed and made holy, so that you can be a useful vessel for God's glory.

   - Invite the Holy Spirit to continue His work in you, making you more like Christ in your thoughts, words, and actions.

4. **Intercession**

   - Pray for those around you, that they may also experience the sanctifying work of the Spirit in their lives.

- Intercede for your church and community, asking God to purify and prepare them for His special purposes.

- Ask God to reveal Himself to those who are in darkness, that they may be turned to the light and receive forgiveness of sins.

5. **Closing Prayer and Commitment**

- Thank God for His sanctifying work and His faithfulness to continue transforming you into His image.

- Commit to walking in greater holiness and obedience, allowing the Holy Spirit to do deeper work in your life.

- Declare that you are an instrument for His special purposes, prepared to do every good work.

Daily Reflections and Insights

Today's Reflection:
In what areas of your life do you need deeper sanctification and cleansing?

Prayer Insight:
How can you allow the Holy Spirit to work more deeply in your life and prepare you for greater service to God?

Commitment Journal:
Write down one area in which you will seek deeper sanctification today:

1.

Day 95: Renewal from Repentance

1. **Opening Worship**

   - Worship God for His grace and mercy, inviting His presence into your life.

   - Thank Him for His invitation to repentance, where He offers forgiveness, renewal, and restoration.

2. **Scripture Meditation**

   - Isaiah 30:15 – Reflect on God's call to repentance and trust in Him, recognising that in repentance, you find true salvation and strength.

   - Luke 5:31-32 – Thank Jesus for His grace toward sinners, understanding that He came to call us to repentance and healing.

   - Acts 3:19 – Pray for a heart of repentance, that God would wipe away your sins and bring times of refreshing and renewal into your life.

3. **Personal Prayers**

   - Ask God to reveal areas in your life where you need to repent and turn back to Him.

   - Confess any sin or struggle, and seek His forgiveness, trusting that He will cleanse and restore you.

   - Pray for a renewed sense of peace, rest, and strength as you respond to God's call to repentance.

4. **Intercession**

   - Pray for those who are far from God, that they would experience the call to repentance and find forgiveness in Christ.

- Intercede for your church, community, and nation, that they would turn to God in repentance, seeking His renewal and transformation.

- Ask God to bring revival and times of refreshing to those who have been weighed down by sin, offering them freedom and healing.

5. Closing Prayer and Commitment

- Thank God for His endless mercy and grace, and commit to turning from sin and embracing His ways.

- Declare that you will seek repentance as a path to renewal, trusting that God will refresh your heart and spirit.

- Commit to living in the peace and strength that come from trusting God's call to repentance.

Daily Reflections and Insights

Today's Reflection:
In what areas of your life do you need to turn back to God in repentance and seek His forgiveness?

Prayer Insight:
How does the promise of renewal from repentance impact your view of God's grace and your own struggles with sin?

Commitment Journal:
Write down one specific sin or area of disobedience you will repent of today and seek God's renewal:

1.

Day 96: More Grace for Continued Obedience

1. **Opening Worship**

   - Praise God for His abundant grace that sustains and empowers you.

   - Worship Him for His faithfulness in providing everything you need to walk in obedience to Him.

2. **Scripture Meditation**

   - Romans 1:5 – Reflect on the grace you have received through faith in Christ, which calls you to obedience for His name's sake.

   - 2 Corinthians 9:8 – Thank God for His abundant blessings, asking Him to empower you to abound in every good work.

   - 2 Corinthians 12:9 – Acknowledge that God's grace is sufficient for you, especially in times of weakness, and that His power is made perfect in your dependence on Him.

3. **Personal Prayers**

   - Ask God to continue giving you the grace to walk in obedience to His will, even in difficult circumstances.

   - Pray for a heart that desires to obey God in all things, trusting that He will supply everything you need for His work.

   - Seek God's strength in moments of weakness, knowing that His grace is more than enough to carry you through.

4. **Intercession**

- Pray for those in your church and community who may be struggling with obedience, that they would experience God's grace and power to continue walking in faith.

- Intercede for leaders and ministers who need God's grace to remain faithful and obedient to their calling.

- Ask God to pour out His grace on the world, that many would come to know Christ and experience the obedience that comes from faith.

5. Closing Prayer and Commitment

- Thank God for His continual grace and provision, and commit to living a life of obedience to His calling.

- Declare that you will rely on His grace in every situation, trusting that His power will be made perfect in your weaknesses.

- Commit to walking in faith, knowing that God's grace will enable you to abound in good works for His glory.

Daily Reflections and Insights

Today's Reflection:
In what areas of your life do you need God's grace to continue in obedience?

Prayer Insight:
How does knowing that God's grace is sufficient in your weaknesses encourage you to keep walking faithfully?

Commitment Journal:
Write down one specific area where you will rely on God's grace to obey Him today:

1.

Day 97: Experiencing the Joy of the Lord

1. **Opening Worship**

    - Thank God for the joy that comes from knowing Him and being in relationship with Him.

    - Worship Him for the hope and peace that overflow through the power of the Holy Spirit, even in trials.

2. **Scripture Meditation**

    - James 1:2-3 – Reflect on how trials test your faith and produce perseverance, leading to pure joy in Christ.

    - 1 Peter 1:8-9 – Praise God for the inexpressible and glorious joy that comes from believing in Jesus, even though you do not see Him.

    - Romans 15:13 – Ask God to fill you with all joy and peace as you trust in Him, and pray for the overflow of hope by the Holy Spirit in your life.

3. **Personal Prayers**

    - Ask God to deepen your understanding of joy, especially in the midst of trials, knowing that your faith is being strengthened.

    - Pray for a heart that overflows with joy, regardless of circumstances, trusting in God's faithfulness and love.

    - Seek God's peace and hope in areas of your life where joy may be lacking, and ask for the Holy Spirit's power to bring joy even in difficult times.

4. **Intercession**

- Pray for those in your church and community who are struggling with joy, that they would experience the joy of the Lord, even in the midst of hardship.

- Intercede for those in pain or sorrow, asking that they would encounter God's peace and joy, knowing He is their refuge.

- Ask God to bring an overflow of hope, joy, and peace to your family, friends, and the world around you.

5. **Closing Prayer and Commitment**

- Thank God for the joy that comes through faith in Jesus Christ and commit to living a life marked by His joy.

- Commit to sharing the joy of the Lord with others, letting it overflow to those around you.

Daily Reflections and Insights

Today's Reflection:
In what areas of your life do you need the joy of the Lord to strengthen and sustain you?

Prayer Insight:
How does your understanding of joy change when you view it as a result of faith and perseverance through trials?

Commitment Journal:
Write down one way you will seek to experience and share the joy of the Lord today:

1.

Day 98: Jesus on the Throne of Our Hearts

1. **Opening Worship**

   - Praise Jesus for being the King who sits on the throne of your heart and for His guidance through the Holy Spirit.

   - Worship Him for the glory He deserves, and declare your heart's desire to honour Him in all things.

2. **Scripture Meditation**

   - John 16:13-14 – Reflect on the role of the Holy Spirit as the One who leads you into all truth and glorifies Jesus. Thank God for His presence in your life and the truth He reveals to you.

   - Luke 24:30-32 – Meditate on the powerful moment when Jesus revealed Himself through the Scriptures and how your heart burns with love and devotion when He speaks.

   - Romans 8:18-19 – Reflect on the future glory that awaits, and how your current sufferings cannot compare to the glory God will reveal. Be filled with hope as you anticipate the revealing of God's glory in your life and the world.

3. **Personal Prayers**

   - Ask Jesus to reign fully in your heart, removing any distractions or things that compete with His lordship.

   - Pray for the Holy Spirit to guide you into deeper truth, revealing more of Jesus' glory to you each day.

   - Ask for the burning passion in your heart that comes from encountering Jesus through His Word, desiring to follow Him with a wholehearted devotion.

   - Seek the strength to endure any trials, trusting that the glory to come is far greater than anything you face now.

4. Intercession

- Pray for your family, church, and community, that they would recognise Jesus as the rightful King of their hearts and allow Him to reign in their lives.

- Intercede for those struggling to fully embrace Jesus as Lord, asking that the Holy Spirit would open their eyes to His glory and truth.

- Pray for the world, that creation would eagerly await the revealing of God's glory, and that many would come to know Jesus as King.

5. Closing Prayer and Commitment

- Thank God for the promise of the Holy Spirit's guidance and for the anticipation of the glory to be revealed in Christ.

- Commit to allowing Jesus to reign on the throne of your heart and to follow His guidance in all things.

- Declare that you will live today with the knowledge of His sovereignty, seeking His truth and glorifying Him in everything.

Daily Reflections and Insights

Today's Reflection:
How can you invite Jesus to sit more fully on the throne of your heart today?

Prayer Insight:
In what ways can the Holy Spirit guide you into deeper truth and revelation of Jesus' glory today?

Commitment Journal:

Write down one area in your life where you want Jesus to have more influence and authority:

1.

Day 99: Trusting God Beyond 100 Days

1. **Opening Worship**

   - Praise God for His righteousness and His Word, which is a lamp to our feet and a guide to our lives.

   - Worship Him for His faithfulness and for the blessings that come when we trust in His guidance. Declare your desire to walk according to His ways.

2. **Scripture Meditation**

   - Psalm 119:1-3 – Reflect on the blessedness of those who walk blamelessly according to God's law. Pray for a heart that seeks God fully and obeys His commands.

   - Psalm 119:4-6 – Meditate on the desire to fully obey God's precepts. Ask God to strengthen your obedience so that you do not experience shame, but walk in His righteousness.

   - Psalm 119:7-9 – Reflect on the commitment to praise God for His righteous laws. Pray for the strength to live according to His Word, especially in areas where you face temptation or struggle.

3. **Personal Prayers**

   - Ask God for a steadfast heart, one that seeks Him with all your heart and follows His ways with integrity.

   - Pray for the courage to obey His statutes, even when it's difficult, trusting that His commands lead to life.

   - Seek God's help in living according to His Word, especially in areas where you feel weak or tempted to stray.

- Pray for spiritual renewal and growth, so that you can walk with Him in purity and holiness, staying on the path He has set before you.

4. Intercession

- Pray for others, asking that they too may walk in the fullness of God's Word, seeking Him wholeheartedly and walking blamelessly.

- Intercede for your church and community, that they would be strengthened in their commitment to live according to God's ways.

- Pray for the world, that many would come to understand the blessings of following God's Word and live in obedience to His commands.

5. Closing Prayer and Commitment

- Thank God for His Word, which guides and strengthens us. Commit to living in full obedience, trusting His instructions even beyond these 100 days.

- Declare that you will continue to seek God with all your heart and follow His ways, knowing that His commands bring blessing and peace.

Daily Reflections and Insights

Today's Reflection:
How has trusting God's Word in the last 100 days impacted your daily decisions?

Prayer Insight:
In what areas of your life do you feel God is calling you to deeper trust and obedience?

Commitment Journal:

Write down 5 ways you will intentionally follow God's Word more closely today and beyond:

1.

2.

3.

4.

5.

Day 100: The Finishing Grace

1. **Opening Worship**

   - Praise God for His grace, love, and the fellowship of the Holy Spirit, which sustain us through every season of life.

   - Worship Him for His faithfulness, and thank Him for the strength He provides to finish the race and stay faithful to His calling.

2. **Scripture Meditation**

   - 2 Corinthians 13:14 – Reflect on the grace of the Lord Jesus, the love of God, and the fellowship of the Holy Spirit. Thank God for these gifts, and ask Him to deepen your experience of them as you continue your journey.

   - 2 Timothy 4:7-8 – Meditate on Paul's declaration of finishing the race and keeping the faith. Pray for the perseverance to fight the good fight, finishing your race with faithfulness, and eagerly longing for the reward that awaits.

   - Acts 20:24-25 – Reflect on the commitment to finish the task that God has given you. Pray that your life would be marked by a single focus: completing the work He has entrusted to you, whether in ministry or daily life.

3. **Personal Prayers**

   - Ask God for the strength to finish well in every aspect of your life, faithfully walking in obedience to His call.

   - Pray for endurance to keep fighting the good fight, even when challenges arise, knowing that the crown of righteousness awaits those who persevere.

- Seek God's grace to remain faithful and diligent in your mission and calling, fulfilling the work He has given you with joy and conviction.

4. Intercession

- Pray for others, asking that they would experience God's finishing grace and remain faithful to their callings.

- Intercede for your church and ministry leaders, that they would finish their race with faithfulness, testifying to God's grace and the power of the gospel.

- Pray for the global Church, that the message of God's grace would be boldly proclaimed to all corners of the earth, and that many would come to know the truth and the hope found in Christ.

5. Closing Prayer and Commitment

- Thank God for His grace that has carried you this far and will continue to lead you in the future.

- Commit to finishing your race with steadfast faith, knowing that Christ's grace is sufficient to keep you to the end. Declare your determination to complete the task He has set before you with His strength, for His glory.

Daily Reflections and Insights

Today's Reflection:
How can you press on in faith and finish well, knowing that God's grace is sufficient for you?

Prayer Insight:
What does the "crown of righteousness" mean to you, and how does it motivate you to continue in your journey of faith?

Commitment Journal:

Write down three areas of your life where you want to finish the race with greater focus and endurance:

1.

2.

3.

Printed in Dunstable, United Kingdom